Christian Uncertainties

By the same author:

WITH LOVE TO THE CHURCH

TRAVELLING IN

CONTEMPLATING NOW

THE END OF OUR EXPLORING

MERTON: A BIOGRAPHY

Christian Uncertainties

by

Monica Furlong

COWLEY PUBLICATIONS
CAMBRIDGE, MASSACHUSETTS

©1975, 1982 by Monica Furlong
This is a reprint of the edition originally published by Hodder &
Stoughton, London, 1975.

International Standard Book Number: 0-936384-06-9
                          previously: 0 340 20130 4
Library of Congress Catalog Number: 82-072129

Published in the United States of America by Cowley Publications
Printed by Shea Brothers, Inc.
Cover design by James Madden, SSJE

Contents

IV PRAYER AND PRE-PRAYER

V THE FOUR LAST THINGS

VI SEVEN UNCERTAINTIES

Preface

WHEN *Christian Uncertainties* came out in 1975 a radio reviewer noted that it was published in the same week as Archbishop Donald Coggan's *Convictions,* a book with a very different attitude. The reviewer's point was that between us we covered two traditional approaches to the Christian faith, the position of 'not knowing' and the position of 'knowing'.

I expect it is possible to make too much of such a difference. Archbishops are paid to 'know' in a way that the laity are mercifully spared, and in any case 'knowing' and 'not knowing' only receive meaning from their opposites. I would have to admit, thought, that I am not very interested in 'convictions', that the fascination of Christianity is not what I know but what I don't know, like the figure that the sculptor perceives in the uncarved block. Christianity appears to me as a religion of few certainties, perhaps only of one — that the pattern of crucifixion and resurrection is cut through the middle of our lives. If we have eyes to see and hearts to feel, it is difficult to live a day without knowing it.

Our principal temptation, I believe, and ironically it is more of a temptation for religious people than for others, is to say that it cannot be like this, mainly because the paradoxes it thrusts upon us are intolerable to our need for comfort and tidy-mindedness. So, casting about for relief from the contradiction of the opposites, we select a solution which we hope will release us; we may choose morality as the key to our escape, or social or political action, or contemplative withdrawal, or the simple, unmaterialistic life, or the life of the private emotions, or art, or heroic self-sacrifice. By one or another of these 'decent' devices we will obtain justification.

I have nothing against any of these paths in themselves, only when they become the answer which lifts us out of the humiliation of the human condition and into a situation in which we are somehow forever safe, right, superior, 'knowing better'. Those of us who took to religion at an early age perhaps are those who suffer a particular temptation to 'know better'. Hating the knowledge of our own frailty, of the permanent wrongness that is built in to the human condition like a family curse, we yearn to find a way of rising above it. This is an unconscious exploitation of Christianity and contrives to miss its whole marvellous point — the creative conflict, the death by way of self-knowledge, shame, despair, lack of self-esteem, and the subsequent rising with the Christ who knows and loves us still. The wholeheartedly sensual usually get to this point before us, as the harlots go first into the kingdom of heaven, because the senses keep men and women more straightforwardly in touch with their own appetites, and appetites have their own humorous way of reminding us of our frailty.

I do not see Christian allegiance as a matter of adopting simple answers and I distrust those who thrust them upon others, particularly if they are urging various kinds of heroic behaviour which the speakers are not required to practise themselves — the heterosexual urging sexual abstinence on the homosexual, celibate priests urging married women not to use contraceptives, or the happily married condemning divorce. Moral 'tidiness' which forces heartbreak or concealment upon others is too cheap for those who recommend it. Only the kind of compassion which includes a careful listening to the problems of others, a listening which by its very nature does not have a simple answer waiting up its sleeve, can possibly do justice either to the complexity of the human situation, or to the deep contradiction or 'tornness' which is at the heart of the crucifixion pattern. Those in pain know very well whether they are being given that sort of attention, or the sort that seeks to bend them to another's will and gratify another's sense of power.

I suppose it was in an attempt to make some such point as this that I originally wrote these pieces for the *Church Times,* the major Anglican publication in Britain. Up to the time of being asked to do them, I had written about religion either in the secular press or for secular publishers and I enjoyed, for a change, writing for a readership accustomed to Christian language, and for whom fewer preliminary explanations were necessary. This was lucky, since the space available was short and there was no room for spelling out complicated histories of ancient disputes.

The response was volatile. Some of the articles caused a good deal of annoyance, with readers writing to abuse me personally and to cancel their subscriptions. But there were also many warm and appreciative letters, often of a touchingly confiding nature, and in some circles the book became popular in church discussion groups as a way of sparking off lively discussion.

What is always fun for a writer is to look back over a passage of time and see how her thinking has changed. Inevitably there are glimpses of old prejudices which now seem rather dated, hints of erstwhile infatuations (now mercifully passed, though others may have taken their place), and touching recollections of the background to particular pieces. What suprises me in these articles is my slowness to see the crucial importance of feminism within the churches, and this is the moment to say that I owe the change in my thinking very largely to the American example. Two long visits to the United States in 1978 and 1979 and a number of shorter visits since have shown me how naturally women take up the task of priesthood, and what an enrichment it is for them and for others. Their help was succeeded by that of friends in England, particularly by Dr. Una Kroll, and all of them together brought me to a new feeling for what the feminine, released from scorn and contempt, might do for the Church and the world.

Feminism, however, is no more an answer than any other 'ism', merely a precious and timely shift of emphasis. I suppose if I were writing some of these pieces now I would make more of what I think of as equilibrium, a point of balance between the opposites which pull at us. Keeping our equilibrium sometimes in real pain, or fear, or anxiety, or any of the states which the word 'disgrace' might properly describe, takes a certain sort of lightheartedness, of humour, of poise, of insouciance. It needs laughter, and the sort of proportion which comes from not taking our lives and our egos too seriously. There is an absurdity in our situation which it is therapeutic to perceive, and of which religion is sometimes splendidly aware; only by its help can we avoid desperate solemnity. If there is one thing I'd like to achieve, it is to make that absurdity clearer.

Monica Furlong
London, 1982

1

SIX KINDS OF LOVING

1: Love of Oneself

CHRISTIANS BELIEVE THAT the transforming agent in human relationships is that of love. It must be the real thing — substitutes won't do; and since most of us are only fitfully capable of generous love, the Christian spiritual 'progress' is one of moving towards a state of loving — not so much learning how to do it as trying to relax into it.

These articles are an attempt to think about that 'progress'; to try to see what stops us relaxing, and also (but much more tentatively because I know much less about it) to see what that state of relaxation is like.

Why is it so hard to love — our neighbours, enemies, children, parents, spouses and friends? Now and again, of course, it is marvellously easy; there are moments of heavenly closeness, sympathy, tenderness, warmth, when we are lifted right out of the loneliness that is the curse of our condition. We discover all over again that we are, as Arnold says, 'parts of a single continent.'

But very often it isn't like that at all, and though there is also a sort of sham loving — what a friend of mine calls 'playing happy families', an attempt to cover the cracks with Christian wallpaper — the cracks are there all right. Bitterness, resentment, anger, envy, spite, afflict Christians no less than other people — in fact I sometimes think rather worse than other people (see the correspondence columns of Christian newspapers, to look no further), just because they guiltily try to bottle them up.

We want to 'be good', and it is painful to have to remember

that we hate quite as much as we love; that like our betters the saints, we wrestle daily with humiliating devils. Yet, when we do recognise this it is a kind of liberation. I find that the friends in whose love I feel most secure are those who know best what seething volcanoes they are inside. Since they don't pretend to feel loving towards me all the time, I know that when they do act lovingly, it is genuine.

Knowing that one hates is part of loving, and so is knowing that a lot of the time we see our fellow-humans not 'as parts of a single continent' (the human) but as deadly rivals. We are infants playing on the floor of God's nursery, full of jealousy about the distribution of the toys, and constantly trying to read the signs whether he loves us more than the others. In this desolate mood no love is possible.

There is our infernal pride, too. Merton says that the 'worship of the self is the last and most difficult of idolatries to detect and get rid of'. We cling on reverently to that fragile little identity we have invented for ourselves, afraid of what? The contempt of others, possession by others, merging with others, desertion by others, total disintegration?

No doubt all the injuries we have sustained since childhood make us afraid to throw away this 'comfort blanket', yet this false identity and the worship of the self that accompanies it make it harder for us to love others than anything else. Hate very often yields to love in the miraculous alchemy of the spirit, but pride never yields to love. It is 'too good' for it — i.e., love is too dangerous to something so precarious.

What is the cure for the idolatry of the self? I suggest that the first step is love of the self. Pride does not come from secretly thinking one is a fine fellow, but from secretly thinking one is a contemptible worm. If others knew *how* contemptible — so runs the inner voice — they would reject me, so I must, I *must* keep up a front, of assurance, meekness, amiability, goodness, industry, or whatever it happens to be.

To love the self means to surrender such costly acting and to pay attention to the real situation: the battered baby within each one of us who does need our care and our patience. It means refusing to condemn or punish ourselves, to find ourselves contemptible and disgusting, but on the contrary gentling ourselves along through all the ups and downs of existence with real charity of heart, finding ourselves touching, funny, interesting and attractive, as we would a real child.

It means giving body, mind and spirit the 'living space' and the 'playing space' that they need – that is to say, refusing to overwork or go without the stimulus or the solitude we may need for health, no matter how much others try to bully or shame or pressurise us into doing so. It means believing in ourselves as going concerns who do not have to justify ourselves; we *are* justified.

We are not awfully good at it. Many of us practice a systematic cruelty on ourselves — more particularly in the matter of overwork — which would be described as sadistic if we did it to anyone else. The Christian excuse for this is often that it is to 'help others', but it begins to sound rather hollow. The people who 'help', at any rate in Western society, are not so much those who wear themselves to a frazzle as those who can 'be there', who can respond freshly and with attention — something impossible for the overtired.

I suggest that love begins with loving oneself and that to achieve this means, for some Christians at this point of time, the surrender of a romantic ideal, that of 'helping others'. My hope is that we may learn to relax into something ultimately of much greater value; that of knowing that we are inextricably part of the others, and not a mite stronger, abler, wiser, better-informed or less in need of help ourselves.

Then we shall be released, anyhow in part, from the idolatry of the self, and free to notice our brothers and sisters.

2: Love in the Family

THERE ARE TWO kinds of human family: the kind that depends on blood kinship, and the kind that depends upon community of interest, ideals or belief. All of us need the first kind for our existence, and usually for our survival. Most of us, certainly all Christians, have some experience of the second kind. This article is mainly about the first kind of family.

I am not one of those who can emote about the family being the keystone of our national life. I am not at all sure that, such a thing being possible, the tribe might not give children more security and less of a hot-house climate to grow up in; but failing that, I am for the family.

It has one splendid characteristic that no 'gathered' collection of people can have, and that is that you belong to it just because you belong. Nobody picks you, and you don't pick yourself. It doesn't matter how old you are or how young, how stupid or clever, how nice or nasty, how neurotic or normal, how orthodox or unorthodox, how virtuous or wicked; you remain related to the members of your family group, and, though they can send you to Coventry, they can't actually deny the connection.

This can, of course, be pretty maddening in practice. It may be hell to have a fascist uncle, an aunt who is a religious maniac, a cousin who is cruel to cats, and a dad who is on the bottle. Worse than that — much worse — our relatives may be bores of the first water, only tolerable at weddings on account of the champagne; yet we are obliged to see them from time to time and even find unnerving resemblances in them to ourselves.

But the forced charity of the family has a kind of beauty about it. We help, and are helped by, our relatives. We resent, and are grateful for, their interest. We put up with embarrassments and foibles that we would never endure for five minutes in a friend, but they do the same for us. We know all their failings and weaknesses right back to infancy; and, what is worse, they know ours. Our mutual knowledge forbids us any fancy idealism about the human race, but replaces it with something better — a real perception of the generations of man, and the way we are indissolubly part of our ancestors and of one another.

And, though family life makes rose-coloured spectacles impossible to wear, it has astonishing moments of warmth and love and concern — moments when a hug or a kiss or a sympathetic gesture or a word lift us or another through some crisis or tragedy and make it possible to continue.

The closest and often the most fraught of family relationships is that between parents and children. All loving relationships have one crucial problem to face — that of the freedom of those related; and it is particuarly difficult in the case of parents and children just because the children have been helpless and dependent for so long that parents get into the habit of being in a position of strength and authority. As the children grow, therefore, so must the parents, just as miraculously and demandingly, except that theirs is an inner growth.

If children are, as it were, to come into their kingdom, then they can only do so by their parents being willing first to assume and then gradually to relinquish authority, all the time knowing inwardly how uncertain and ambivalent they are over even their most cherished beliefs. (At least I hope they know that.)

If we relinquish power too soon, or refuse ever to assume our position of seniority ('People take us for sisters!') then the young may be forced to seek it in some ideology or belief that supplies all answers, however rashly and simplistically. If, on the other hand, we hold on to power too long, or present it in too heavy-handed a way, then our children may never grow out of a timid compliance — never, in fact, grow up at all.

Timing is of supreme importance — we can only yield power to our children when they know how to ask us for it; and we often have to listen very hard to catch that request. What we are hoping for, it seems to me, is that our children will learn to act upon truth — their own truth, not necessarily ours — while knowing something of how paradoxical it is, perhaps even contradictory.

Parents must, in a sense, abdicate if children are to find their inheritance; and it is a complex and difficult business this handing over of the parental kingdom to the young, perhaps only possible where love is deeply and permanently established. *King Lear* stands as a terrible warning of how it may be done brutally, suicidally, inviting (and getting) a cruel response. A more loving and less sick father than Lear might have moved slowly, watching carefully to see how his children moved free of him in the world, giving generously but careful of his own self-respect, his own need for richness.

Lear is a dreadful, but pathetic, old man. Need old age, despite the loss of strength and power, always have pathos? I don't believe it.

Where religion has had something precious to say about age, it has been because it knows that it is not simply a loss and a humiliation but also a freedom. Released from the heavy burden of making money, running a family and doing an exacting job, the religious man has the sort of poverty he needs to give him inner space, whether or not he is living on a decent income.

And, if he can use his inner freedom to give others freedom, then he is sure of being loved, by his own family among others.

3: Love in Marriage

OF ALL HUMAN attempts to put love into practice, none perhaps is as brave or ambitious as marriage. To live with one other person for a lifetime, to make them one's only sexual partner, to have and bring up children by them, to remain loyal to them through the many crises which beset the human condition, is a very demanding programme; and it is not surprising that many fail to a greater or lesser degree.

It is an 'ordinary' spiritual discipline, one simply and often beautifully undertaken by thousands of people with no spiritual pretensions, and it is moving to see the effect that years of love and loyalty and devotion can have on the character of those who are thoroughly and deeply married. They are not necessarily always happy. 'Good' marriages, it seems to me, go through darknesses, moments of real renunciation, times when the other must be given up — unpossessed, as it were — in order to be rediscovered. Like the couple in *The Magic Flute* real lovers undergo ordeals, baffling experiences in which all that they thought they knew about life may have to be unlearned and learned anew.

It is this learning experience, this shattering of pre-conceptions, that love is about. Love is an awesome and terrible experience, an operation performed on the soul that is no less than total in its final transformation; and, though marriage, like religious ritual, is an attempt to contain this creative terror in a bearable (i.e. a familiar) form, there will still be moments — in sexual ecstasy, in childbirth, in illness, in grief, in joy — when deep wonder may overwhelm a couple. It is not surprising that boredom — in human beings so often the mask of fear — is a problem in marriage as it is a problem in prayer.

Apart from the numinosity of love, it is a fearful thing to know and be known by one other person in depth. In the beginning the wealth of sharing is a delight and a wonderful relief of loneliness. But beyond this there is a level on which it is difficult to share for fear of wounding the other or of being humiliated by their knowledge.

It is touching to witness the sensitivity of many married couples towards each other's weaknesses; they often thrive by never putting into words the failures, the temptations, the attractions, the fantasies which plague them or which they know very well plague their partner. A few remarkable couples can share everything — even the darkest and sickest corners of their minds; but this requires a self-knowledge, a humility and a spiritual resource in both partners that few people actually have.

Of course closeness and sharing make wounding an ever-present possibility. Married couples can hurt one another as no one else could hurt either of them. Probably only the brave admission of the wish to hurt — that is to say, of the hate locked up in love — can get a couple through that particular dark wood.

All marriages worthy of the name go through considerable ups and downs; it is no light thing to live with another person, however dearly we love them; but no one who has once understood it can doubt the value of 'sticking with' a marriage through all its difficulties.

But what of marriages that don't work at all? There is a disturbing Christian tendency to say that there is no such thing as a marriage that doesn't work; a belief that, if you say 'It *must* work' often enough, then the wish will govern the reality. I am bound to say that I don't believe this is necessarily true; that a couple may marry in church in the hope of making a good marriage and fail totally, either because their personalities interact in a deeply destructive way or because in some puzzling sense, the marriage is, as it were, still-born, psychologically lifeless.

Christian unwillingness to admit this kind of possibility has made us inhibited about discussing marital failure among Christians, and the whole subject is still hedged about with fears and taboos and dogma; but at least one aspect is worth thinking about. Which is that, though the age of marriages of convenience in the old sense is dead, many people, particularly in youth, still marry as a result of pressure rather than of loving commitment. The pressures are hidden and subtle, and often pitifully silly, but they are there none the less, working against the genuine growth of love.

I can think of couples I know who married from desperate loneliness, because Mum wanted it, because Mum didn't want it, to get away from home, because they wanted a baby, because they were afraid of homosexual feelings, because they wanted sex, because their friends were getting married, because they felt sorry for their partners, because they wanted to mother, or *be* mothered (or fathered), and a score of other bad reasons.

Sometimes, in spite of such a rotten start, a marriage still works. But it is not surprising if, in some cases, the basic mistake — a kind of untruthfulness to the self and its needs — cannot be overcome.

Marriage is about growth in love, and I wonder what we do if we condemn someone who makes a mistake at eighteen, or twenty, or twenty-five, to a lifelong sterile relationship. Of course spiritual growth is still, mercifully, possible in conditions of the most extreme deprivation, but it is a terrible thing to impose such conditions upon others; and perhaps, if we really care about marriage, we should be more concerned that it is not founded upon falsity and that it opens the way for men and women to fulfil their potential.

4: Love of Neighbour

I SEEM TO BE worse at loving my neighbour than almost anyone I have ever known — a fact you may like to bear in mind while reading the rest of this article.

It's not so much that I don't like people as that I only feel completely at ease with two kinds of people — those who know me well and those who don't know me at all. The kind of partial knowledge of another person which is subsumed under the heading of 'neighbour' is just the kind of relationship I find most difficult. I am not an easy chatterer to strangers, a natural 'dropper-in' or helper of blind men across streets, nor is mine the kind of friendly face that people are glad to see over the garden fence.

If I sound sensitive on the subject, it is because I have just been reading one of those books which says that the Christian home should be a perpetual refuge for the stranger — the door ever open to the alien and the unloved, the coffee always steaming on the stove, hospitality constantly available along with a listening ear and an understanding heart. *That*, says the book, is how to love one's neighbour — a kind of domestic version of overseas aid. In addition, one should be busy helping the needy and infirm who live round about one.

I don't despise any of that. The alien always interest me; and, at times when I have felt alien myself, I have been glad of others' kindness and hospitality. I can imagine what it means to be served by loving hands in infirmity. It takes, therefore, nerve to say that that is not a version of loving my neighbour which I feel able to make my own.

I *could* not love my neighbour if he was perpetually on my hearth-rug, nor would I be much practical use in anyone's home unless they were absolutely *in extremis*. Perpetual busyness, the constant presence of others, endless demands on my interest and sympathy would, quite simply, drive me barmy, in a way that the extrovert end of Christian practice always finds so hard to believe.

Is there then an alternative method which may be attempted by Christian candidates? I believe that there is, and that we are gradually learning that we must devote as much care and respect to it as to the busy kinds of loving.

The kind of loving I am talking about is one that is rooted in solitude — not total solitude (few can have or could bear, total solitude), but a deliberate choice *not* to be with other people because solitude provides a sort of inner space necessary for growth. This kind of loving has varied expressions — the religious contemplative springs to mind as the most obvious example, but others — the scholar, the artist — can only give whatever it is they have to give to mankind if long periods of their lives are spent alone and without continual interruption.

Of course scholars, artists and contemplatives are in the minority; most of us have to work with other people, and the only thing we have any choice about is what to do with our limited spare time. But I often detect in all sorts of people a real longing for reflective activity, for deeper intuitions, for time in which to discover inner riches. To help and encourage people to undertake this inner growth may be a roundabout way of getting them to love their neighbour, but it is, I believe, part of the Church's vocation.

Suppose some of us try to see what it means to love in solitude; that is to recognise that whatever we have to give others does not seem to emerge by way of extroversion but takes another route? What will we find then?

First, I suppose, the kind of introspection of which the English have always been so intensely suspicious. If we are not continually distracted by others, nor given a pseudo-identity or role by them, we do get to know ourselves rather better — an unnerving experience, one in which we will certainly learn something of depression and inner conflict.

Second, a different layer of concentration, one which, if we practise this kind of love faithfully, ought to make it possible to respond much more freshly to the people and ideas which do come our way. (Contemplative monks and nuns often show this freshness to a marked degree).

Third, an ability to wait, to let go, not to be consumed by 'wanting'.

Fourth, the discovery that it is an illusion that we have anything to give our neighbour except our own being – a gift which he bestows in turn upon us.

Some of us can love others one way, others in another; and probably none of us ever quite knows the extent to which we, or others, are humbugs, the leading characters in our own private fiction. But what in the end is loving our neighbour about — whether we pursue it in the soup-kitchen, the study, the settlement, the studio or the cell? It is about discovering that our funny, precious little identities are a joke; that, instead of being separate, we are one with our neighbour (neither better than him, nor worse) in our mutual failure and loneliness and hope and longing; the name of the oneness being Christ.

5: Love of One's Enemies

NOTHING HARDER IS ever asked of any of us than to love our enemies; in fact it is so difficult that some of us cannot achieve it at all.

It is possible to cheat by not choosing to notice the feelings of anger, revenge, and violence others evoke in us — I have done it on and off for years. We can then appear in our own eyes as loving people; only we usually give the game away by the unkind things we say — either to people's faces or behind their backs, it scarcely matters which. If we are clever people we do it cleverly, and probably amusingly. If we are less clever we do it clumsily. But it causes pain. Hatred has as much necessity to find expression as the mosquito has to sting.

The first step towards loving one's enemies is not the suppression of hateful feelings (as a bastardised Christianity has sometimes taught), but the courageous discovery of them. We are like the Pharisees — good at loving those who love us, but not good at loving those who we feel a threat to us. People who sneer at our beliefs and values, who pour scorn on the people we hold precious, who treat us or others with open or veiled contempt, who ignore us, who laugh at us, or who just appear to us maddeningly wrong-headed, can each and every one of them start our adrenalin going, our hearts pounding, our blood racing. We are ready, animals that we partly are, to fight and destroy in self-defence.

It is painful to discover violent feeling within. Sometimes it seems helpful to acknowledge our anger to our adversary. 'I did hate you when you said . . .' often seems to clear the air remarkably, particularly in the closest relationships — not least because the admission nearly always gives useful information. We often do not know when we are arousing anger in others, and they are similarly blind about us.

Personally, I have not moved beyond these foothills to make the Everest attempt of actually loving my enemies; so far it is beyond me. The few people I know who have done so have usually reached this summit under extraordinary pressures of one kind or another.

One of them, for example, was a man whose divorce brought long and bitter recriminations from his ex-wife for many, many years after they had parted. In the beginning he had replied to her hateful accusations in kind, and only gradually did he learn how damaging, and interminable, such exchanges could become. He learned not to engage on fruitless arguments, not to return anger, not to bring up resentments from the past. To learn to refuse not to be goaded — there is a kind of luxury in letting one's anger rip — was for him a great achievement. It might be too much to say that he learned to love her, but he did at least learn not to hate and hurt her.

A more drastic example of loving one's enemies is described in Dumitriu's *Incognito*. Driven to extremes of anger and hatred as a result of his treatment by prison guards, the hero Sebastian knows that he can only survive by making some inner step that he cannot imagine. Suddenly, alone in a filthy cell, the message comes to him: that he must love his enemies. His new discovery is terribly tried in the months which follow.

'I had to struggle not to sink below the level of love and fall back into the realm of hatred, anger and revenge; to love Romulus Luca, not for a moment but continuously. I had to drive my soul to do this as one may push a vehicle with locked brakes.'

He finds that this effort gives him a deep understanding of his enemy and the twisted emotions which drive him. It also has the unexpected effect that he can love those whom he already loved with a new intensity; and this in turn leads to a new realisation of Christ, 'the one who had most deeply and intensely loved . . . the first of a future mankind wherein a mutation of human hearts will in the end cause the Kingdom of God.'

Most of us do not suffer as Sebastian suffered, and so are not pushed to this ultimate discovery; we can avoid our enemies, or, at any rate, dilute our anger with pleasanter experiences. We may never learn to do very much more than be honest with ourselves about our emotions — in itself no easy or comforting task. But at the root of Sebastian's experience, or our own, one thing remains true, though we are only fleetingly aware of it. It is that we *are* our brother.

'It may sometimes happen,' wrote one of the Hasidic rabbis, 'that thine own hand inadvertently strikes thee. Wouldst thou take a stick and chastise thy hand for its heedlessness, and thus add to thy pain? It is the same when thy neighbour, whose soul is one with thine, does thee harm: shouldst thou retaliate, it would be thou who wouldst suffer.'

6: The Love of God

THE LOVE OF God, over the centuries, has found expression in all sorts of ways, many of them inspiring to contemplate.

To look no further than the Christian consciousness of God, it has summoned men to sublime feats of love, of art, of learning, to disciplines that have immeasurably enriched the consciousness of mankind. I do not see how anyone can fail to be grateful when he finds himself the heir of such beauty. I can think of paintings, of sculpture, of cathedrals and churches I have seen, of liturgy in which I have taken part, which have summoned me out of my limited, impoverished self to riches I had not guessed at.

Yet, although some people in our time still create from religious feeling, I am not at all sure that this is, so to speak, where the action is at. I could be very wrong about this — I know many Christian friends will disagree with me — but I do not think we shall be ready again for the unselfconsciousness out of which living art and liturgy come until we have gone through another process or series of processes first.

It is risky to derive too much from historical analogies; but, when I try to think about our present spiritual condition, there is one historical situation that recurs in my mind so frequently that I cannot resist sharing my thoughts on the subject. That is the story of the Exodus. The Old Testament, like so much ancient literature, is full of people mysteriously summoned upon costly journeys; but Jewish literature is particularly marked with the awareness that it is God who issues the summons, as well as God who *is*, in a sense, the journey itself.

For the Jews the agonising decision to set off into the wilderness came out of a spiritual, mental and physical impoverishment that had become intolerable. With the dreadful human capacity to bear suffering long past the point where it should be

borne they had carried on not so much from conviction about
what they did as from terror of the alternative, the giving up of
all that they knew, and the going out into the unknown. They
could never have done it without Moses, a man God-conscious
beyond the normal, but even with his help they had fearful
doubts and backslidings.

In retrospect they and their descendants saw the agonising
decision to leave, and the traumatic events which followed, as
the most important thing that ever happened to them ('their
finest hour,' as another leader put it). At the time, no doubt,
they grieved over leaving the cat behind and not seeing the
garden at its best: such is the human way of experiencing great
events in tiny, searing details.

My point in comparing their condition to ours is that the
wilderness seems, once again, to beckon in a way that it has not
done through all the 'Christian centuries' of our past, unless
perhaps the Desert Fathers were responding to a similar crisis.
(Not that I see our solution as being as literal as theirs). Unlike
our Christian ancestors we find ourselves in poverty, not 'knowing' what to do, but waiting, waiting, for the moment in which
the unknown beckons us out. It is a terribly unnerving experience, one in which, so it seems to me, none of the usual aids
quite works.

We cannot rely on law (the experience itself creates the law),
nor on tradition (we are ourselves the tradition), nor on authority (no one has passed this way before). We can rely on nothing
but our faith in God; and every single thing we took for
granted — whether moral, physical, or spiritual — may turn out
to be too heavy to carry with us. In the miraculous light of the
desert we have to consent to be fed directly from God's hand
like babies; our pride and self-sufficiency has to be sacrificed,
along with much else.

If we are prepared to undergo this archetypal experience
then we shall again become a people (though an unrecognisably
different people), and being a people we will again forge a
language, an ethic and an art.

The danger is, always, that we may try to use our religion not to lead us out into the terrifying desert but to keep us safe in Egypt, where we may be degraded and depressed past endurance but where our bellies are more or less full. 'I wish,' says God wistfully in the Talmud, 'they would forsake me, and observe my teachings.' 'The teachings' are a calling of us into creativity, into new ideas, new thought-forms, new ways of fulfilling our potential; and, if we use God to stifle our creativity or that of others, we are lost.

The Jews used to talk of the Shekhinah, the Presence of God, the Glory, which was lost and dissipated in the world until the soul of man was prepared to take it into itself to bring about redemption. It is that glory which, once again, we have lost; we can feel the loss of it in our language, our art, our liturgy. Once again we have to go in search of it, and find it waiting for us in the wilderness.

II
THE SEVEN DEADLY SINS

1: The Seven-Finger Exercise

PRIDE, WRATH, ENVY, lust, gluttony, sloth and avarice have always seemed to me a rather sparse account of human wickedness and folly. Hypocrisy now, what about that? Or cruelty? Or prejudice?

But the point about the Seven Deadly Sins perhaps is that they are the usual ones, the ones that all of us commit. Not everyone is a hypocrite or a bigot; that takes a certain perverse talent. But all of us, unfortunately, find the deadly seven-finger exercise well within our range. We have its bizarre tune 'on the brain'; and, just when we think we have got rid of it and are now ready to listen to something nicer, its insidious variations creep back and take possession of us all over again. It is a 'normal' form of pathology.

But that is no comfort since the sins, and the gamut of emotions which accompany them, are deeply destructive. We tend, when talking about sin, to talk of the damage it does to others, but the worst damage is to ourselves.

Our forebears were much better at perceiving this than we are. Hieronymus Bosch, in his painting, 'The Seven Deadly Sins', showed the envious man being torn apart by dogs, the lustful man being eaten by wild beasts, the slothful man being cruelly beaten, the angry man undergoing castration. He was, it is true, thinking partly in terms of appropriate punishment, but like a masturbation fantasy, his artistic fantasies gave clues as to where the root of the suffering lay. Each sin was a desperate form of suicide, a heartrending cry to be delivered from the body of this living death.

At the root of every sin is a kind of hopelessness — a hopelessness which springs from the fear that we are nothing and nobody, that nobody loves us and wants us, that nothing good will ever again happen to us. Impossible to sustain life in such a vacuum, so we take one of seven deluded steps to what we hope will be fulfilment, to that state of being loved, and accepted, and wanted, and admired, which is our rainbow's end.

If you examine the seven deadly sins carefully, what a number of them have in common is a wish to manipulate life — even, in the case of envy, to control it by a sort of magic. 'If I want something hard enough, I will get it.' Avarice and gluttony strive to keep an elusive security always within their own grasp. Wrath and lust select instead the *tour de force*, using feeling as a way of trying to take fulfilment by storm.

What all of these sins have in common is a memory of infancy with its illusions of omnipotence, its desperate hungers and longings, and its screaming rage when they were not fulfilled. Sloth takes another, more neurotic path; its method of manipulating life is to dodge its hard knocks altogether by not attempting to live it. Pride, the most contemptible of the sins, is another kind of dodging; it is a pretence that one is different, special, exempt from the ordinary human lot of hurt and shame and failure; a quisling betrayal of oneself and one's kind.

Perhaps because there is so much of infancy in our sinning when we are caught out, or catch ourselves out, the sense of shame, of nakedness, is very painful indeed. It is as if we are reduced to four years old again, caught misbehaving by uncomprehending grown-ups. No wonder we resist the knowledge; justify, defend, excuse ourselves till we are exhausted, while being quick to distract attention from ourselves by pointing at others. It takes the most sensitive of confessors, the most loving of friends, the most skilful of therapists, to lead us to the point of discovering, and bearing, the fact that we are no better than anybody else.

Yet this is the most joyful, the most humorous of all discoveries, ridding us of a frightful weight of pretence. 'I have put down a light burden,' wrote one of the Desert Fathers, 'that of reprehending myself, and taken up a heavy burden, that of condemning others.' Reverse the process, as he was about to do, and there is the relief of admitting that, instead of being perfect, as we would like to be, we are cunning, devious children terrified our siblings are going to get our share of love. We are not special, just very human.

And because we are human, only one remedy works for us. In a moving passage of his autobiography Bunyan describes going to church in a state of utter despair at his own sinfulness. He thought nothing could save him from damnation, and repined terribly at the thought of the joy from which he was excluded.

But the preacher spoke of the love of Christ for man, and as Bunyan listened a profound change came over him. He heard a voice within him saying, 'Thou art my love, thou art my love, and nothing shall separate thee from my love.' A sense of forgiveness came over him and of great joy, so that 'I thought I could have spoken of his Love ... even to the very Crows that sat upon the plow'd lands before me.'

Not all of us experience love quite as Bunyan did; it comes to us in many ways and through many relationships as well as by direct religious emotion. Yet however it comes, it seems to be the only thing that can release us from the seven-finger exercise, and attune our ears to a different melody and rhythm.

2: Envy

IF ENVY WERE not such a tearing thing to feel, it would be the most comic of the sins. It is usually, if not always, based on a complete misunderstanding of another person's situation.

We catch a glimpse of their beauty, their talent, their success, their idyllic marriage or their wealth, and build upon it a romanticised structure of happiness which we contrast with our own miserable lot. Perhaps we always half know that we are making it up, but in any case life often teaches us better. When we get to know the subject of our envy better we discover that he is not a superman but vulnerable and sometimes unhappy. In the flash of envy, however, we become temporarily blind to this universal truth.

Envy is the sin of the eyes — something very evident in Bosch's painting of 'Invidia', which is full of people eyeing one another meaningfully and dogs eyeing one another's bones. Not that it only happens by looking, but the gift of sight does make it possible to compare; and comparison is the essence of envy, as in those nauseating advertisements where women worry about whether their children's shirts are whiter or their jumpers better washed than other people's.

The advertisers know us well enough to know that generosity to our contemporaries (i.e. rivals) does not come easily to us. We do not readily think, 'What a marvellous mother!' Rather we think, 'If *she* is a good mother, that makes me a bad mother.'

Buried in envy is a feeling of inferiority and persecution; the world does not understand me, appreciate me, value me, as I would like to be understood and valued, and this causes me intolerable pain. Looking at somebody else who seems to get the admiration I would like, I feel as if they are robbing me. The touching wish to be Somebody which lurks at the bottom of so many of our sins pushes me into competition. Like the child in the nursery I cannot believe that there is room for two of us.

Sin works in two directions, damaging others and damaging ourselves. In the case of envy it changes the others from fallible, foolish creatures much like ourselves into a persecutory 'They' who have all the luck; and it changes us into persecuted people who can never have a feeling of fullness or riches because we are perpetually deprived, always hungry. When envy really gets a grip on us we are full of complaint and seem to lose all capacity for gladness. I have one acquaintance, much afflicted with envy, who even believes that the *weather* is worse where he is than it ever is anywhere else.

Such extreme forms of envy may stem from a real experience of persecution in childhood. Life after all can be grossly unfair, and some people do get more of the good things than others. This does not lead inevitably to envy — some people manage to be unenvious on very little and others just the opposite — but some backgrounds do seem to predispose people to envy.

So, I believe, do other social factors. Women, I sometimes think, tend to be more envious than men: either of other women, as in the advertisements, or, more damagingly, of their own husbands, particularly where they follow a satisfying career and the wife believes her talents have been denied. It is painful to see the poison of married envy seeping out in cutting little remarks designed to diminish the partner. But women have undergone a long and historic battle to become 'Somebody', and it is not surprising if they feel a bit wobbly in their status.

In a perfect Christian world we should all be sublimely indifferent to status, but we have not got so far. As an old priest in a book by Malraux remarks: 'There is no such thing as a grown-up person.' We still have our childish longings to be Somebody, and one way to control envy is to admit that we do want admiration, success and love, and will become impossible if we don't get a certain amount of it. Wiser, perhaps, to acknowledge that we are ambitious, like possessions and want others to find us attractive than to renounce these things as vanities and then pine for what we miss.

In the end, though, no amount of 'having' really cures us, because it never touches, except in the most superficial way, the hunger that causes envy. That envy is only cured by discovering we are Somebody (a discovery we can only make by way of love). When we know we are Somebody, then we can allow others to be Somebodies too; and then, if we are lucky, we see that we have been taken in by a kind of trick, the illusion that we are all separate. Suddenly, though only momentarily, we see that when another person has a joy or a triumph it does not diminish us, in fact quite the contrary.

When everyone is somebody, as Gilbert says, then no one's anybody. This is the most comic and delightful of discoveries, one of which only the saints seem able to take permanent hold. It is when we perceive the farcical nature of the ego that we are finally convinced of the ludicrousness of envy.

3: Gluttony

'WHAT I LIKE about gluttony,' a bishop I once knew used to say, 'is that it doesn't hurt anyone else.' I suppose that, if I had wanted to be crushing I might have come back with some withering retort about the Third World; but I liked his honesty too much for that, and, anyhow, we weren't talking about world economic problems but about our own moral and psychological ones.

He meant that he suffered less guilt as a result of his, fairly modest, over-eating and over-drinking than he did as a result of his other failings; and this indicated, I thought, a sense of proportion as well as a sense of humour. Mild gluttony has something touchingly childlike and human about it; I detest the sort of people who are for ever incapable of it, suspecting in them a contempt for the body and its simple joys.

We are sensual creatures, inextricably bound up in our needs and our longing for bodily pleasure; it is usually better for others when we don't pretend otherwise, as the worst human nastinesses seem to occur when we think we are too good for our bodies. The pleasures of the body are exquisite, as an overweening Christianity has sometimes tried to forget. The joy of good food lovingly cooked, of a fine wine (or even a glass of water or beer when we are thirsty), the delight of sex, the bliss of sleep, are as near to heaven as some of us are capable of imagining.

It is because the pleasures are so good, because they give us their own unique insights into the love and satisfaction which is heaven, that we get into difficulties. How can we let go of this lovely moment of delight, how not seek to prolong it indefinitely?

As it happens, life does not really give us the choice. As a result of what Freud called the 'reality principle' we are forced to surrender our pleasures repeatedly, forced by the need for self-preservation in all its forms. We have to get up on cold Monday mornings and go to work, and day after day face all the lonelinesses and hardships of a competitive world.

It is under the stresses of life that people nowadays are led into gluttony (it may have been otherwise for medieval princes). Feeling unsatisfied by life in general, we turn more compulsively to the kinds of satisfaction that are within our grasp.

The sorts of satisfaction which we are denied may be the satisfaction of interesting work, intellectual stimulus, rewarding companionship, sexual expression, or simple affection; but the child in us resorts to a much more primitive sort of satisfaction, that of eating. So we eat or we drink or we smoke too much, using these habits not as part of a joyous communion with the world about us but as tranquillisers and anaesthetics to deaden our perceptions.

Eating or drinking with delight is oddly different from eating or drinking out of greed. Delight is marked by an un-forced sense of gratitude, by gaiety and humour, by a moment-by-moment awareness of pleasure; finally, by a sort of love that overflows and seems to make everyone and everything in the vicinity beautiful. We are rich. God, you might say, is present.

Greed, by contrast, is earnest and anxious, with the emphasis not on the delight of tasting but on 'getting' the food or drink inside you. There is something solitary and guilty about the compulsion. Impossible for us gluttons to wait for the magic moment when God comes of his own free-will; we want him imprisoned in this bottle (or, more ludicrously still, in the cake-tin or the biscuit-barrel), and so ours to command.

> *He who binds to himself a joy*
> *Doth the wingèd life destroy,*

wrote Blake. Yes, we know about that, and about the self-contempt which follows.

The difficult answer for the glutton (as for all the other kinds of sinner) is that he needs to be loved more. Ultimately this means to become more aware of the love of God, but most of us are bad at this until other human beings demonstrate it to us by the quality of their loving. The glutton needs more of other people's love, yet, in order to receive it, he has to surrender some of his pride and self-sufficiency. He has to make the painful discovery that he is dependent, but that dependency on people is more promising than dependence on things.

It is not only the love of others that he needs, but also love for himself. The glutton has a lot of self-hatred locked up inside him; in fact over-eating and over-drinking can be seen as a slow self-destruction. If he can give himself something of the tender care, the mothering or fathering that he so much lacks, then he may avoid the desperation that drives him to extremes (and which sets off once again the whole cycle of self-contempt.)

Above all, he may stumble upon the lost rhythms of his own body and of the world about him, rediscovering what it means to be an ordinary, needy human being, and content to be so.

> *Always eat when you are hungry,*
> *Always drink when you are dry,*
> *Always close your eyes when sleeping.*
> *Don't stop breathing or you'll die.*

It is a modest, but not contemptible, version of the religious life.

4: Lust

ONE OF THE Desert Fathers, Abbot John, reported triumphantly to his confessor that, after a long struggle, he had finally overcome all passion in himself. His confessor wasn't pleased at all. 'Go back,' he told him, 'and pray to be tempted again.' Like the wise old man that he was he knew that passion, whether of anger or sexual desire, was part of normal human experience; woe to the man who is 'too good' for that sort of thing, since, by pride or repression, he has abdicated his humanity.

You can see why we want to be 'too good' to feel sexual desire. Unsatisfied, it can torment us physically and mentally, filling our minds with troubling fantasies, awakening old wounds and shames. Satisfied, if satisfaction occurs outside the limits of religion or social *mores*, it brings guilt, and possibly fear of disgrace.

In fact it is not easy to live, as a human being must, with being a sexual creature. It is all right for the animals for whom sexual longing is a seasonal frenzy to be satisfied as suddenly, and often as violently, as it occurs. It is much harder for us for whom sex seems to touch upon so many other things — our loyalties to others, our wish for stable family life, our need for social acceptance on the one hand, and our need to grow as individuals, our need for ecstasy, even our longing to find God on the other. Sex lies at the very quick of our lives — in our deepest hope to love and be loved, to heal and to be healed.

It is the tremendous hope that all of us invest in sex which
makes me feel we should be more compassionate to one
anothers' sexual longings than to anything else. (In practice,
however, because of fear and envy, we are just the opposite.)
We are muddled and foolish, and we make terrible mistakes.
Sexual desire then slides easily towards lust, the condition in
which love becomes swallowed in hunger.

Yet, for all our capacity to get it wrong, we do so desperately
want to get it right, knowing even in our lost moments that, if
we *can* get sexual desire and love together in the same place at
the same time, then we have achieved one of the greatest delights of being human, a truly religious moment.

'To know oneself half of a true pair,' writes Dumitriu in
Incognito, 'certain of its purity and integrity, and the whole
encompassed by warmth and tenderness, compassion, pity and
gratitude; this is the only way of overcoming our loneliness,'
except for certain spiritual experiences he goes on to describe.
It is this closeness of the 'true pair' of which lust, with its
perverted fantasies and its tormenting obsessions, is such a pitiful travesty.

Unfortunately wishing to be half of a 'true pair', or even
trying hard, does not necessarily bring it about. Many find close
relationship overwhelmingly difficult. Marriage, the social and
religious remedy for lust, does not always, or perhaps even
often, result in a 'true pair'; probably few of us are capable,
anyhow in youth, of such an achievement; our wounds, and
sins, and sheer lack of experience and understanding work
against our deepest longing. Some people find their 'true pair'
outside the marital bond — a costly discovery in a society which
still sets great store by marital fidelity. Some can only imagine
forming a 'true pair' with someone of their own sex.

I feel that one of the loving things that Christians might do
for our society at the present time is to become much more wise
and gentle and, above all, truthful about what the problems of
relationship between people are, and more particularly about
their own problems. The tendency to talk in ideals makes it
difficult for Christians to admit that they are unhappily mar-

ried, that they have fallen in love outside the marriage bond, or that they prefer homosexual love to heterosexual love; yet, as any confessor knows, Christians have such problems no less than other people. The sacrament of marriage is no magical remedy; and, though it is a beautiful thought that marriage symbolises 'the mystical union that is betwixt Christ and his Church', the gap between the ideal and the reality often reaches farcical proportions.

We live in a society, or rather in a world, where the majority of people find very real difficulties in forming a 'true pair', though their reasons vary enormously. The difficulties mean that most of us, Christian or not, know a good deal about hunger and so about lust; and I think that, unless we can see ways of bettering the human lot, we should be content to be part of suffering humanity in this way.

It is the miracle of salvation that creativity springs not from our strength and virtue but from our weakness, emptiness, and shame. So that lust, if accepted simply, almost humorously, without excuses or justifications, is turned from our crucifixion to our resurrection. 'One of the elders said it is not because evil thoughts come to us we are condemned but only because we make use of the evil thoughts. It can happen that from these thoughts we suffer shipwreck, but it can also happen that because of them we may be crowned.'

5: Sloth

WE HAVE DEBASED the word 'sloth', making it synonymous with laziness, with which it has nothing in common except a state of inactivity. Laziness, nowadays, is an art which many of us need to re-learn. Sloth, on the other hand, is a sort of living death.

The most terrible and moving example of sloth I know occurs in Bruno Bettelheim's book *The Informed Heart*. Writing of Nazi Germany, he describes the vain attempt by himself and others to persuade elderly Jewish relatives to leave the country while there was still time. They knew, from daily experience and from the insistence of the young, that there was no future for them in Germany, yet the fear of giving up all that they had known and venturing into the unknown was too great. They turned inward, clinging to their few possessions, trying to ignore the horror that washed around them until it finally engulfed them.

It is not for us to criticise from our own, far happier, vantage point, yet it is possible to learn from this extreme example something of the paralysis of sloth. Sloth is when one *knows* one is set upon a damaging or deadly course and somehow cannot muster the strength, the courage, the hope, the faith, to do something different. The slothful man is in very great pain — Bosch depicts him as being savagely beaten; yet he does not seem able to move away, to say 'that is enough' and to redirect his life accordingly.

Is this a common sin in our society? Speaking only from observation of people I know and listen to, I think it is very common. The man who detests his job, but continues in it for a lifetime; the woman who sees herself as a martyr to her family; the grown-up child who never really makes the break with father or mother, the married couple whose relationship is a living hell — all these exhibit the deadly marks of sloth.

One thing the slothful all have in common is a perfect alibi. Suggest to them some practical step which might take them only a little way out of their suffering, and they are down on you like a ton of bricks. The man must continue with his drudgery to support his family; the martyred housewife knows her husband and children will be lost without her ministrations; the unhappily married couple have any number of moral and practical reasons for not being able to part, even temporarily.

Bettelheim's relatives were equally certain, ' "How could we leave? It would have meant giving up our homes, our places of business." ' Bettelheim sadly concludes that 'their earthly possessions had so taken possession of them that they could not move; instead of using them, they were run by them'.

But it was not avarice that held them back but fear of the unknown (their possessions representing the known); a fear which they masked in the language of common-sense, of doing the practical thing. With hindsight we know that it was not the practical thing, but perhaps by learning from them we can see how often we use common-sense as an alibi to prevent us from taking the leap of faith that might release us from our suffering. Alternatively, we use morals to save us from faith, protesting that it is 'our duty' not to pursue a different course.

We can guess we are guilty of sloth when we find ourselves continually depressed and in pain but can produce excellent moral and practical reasons why we cannot improve our own lot. A distorted Christianity has sometimes made a virtue out of being in pain, as it has made a virtue out of martyring oneself for a cause. I believe we should reject this masochistic device, and try instead to be happy and live as fully as we can, accepting suffering if it comes (as it does anyway) but becoming intensely suspicious of our motives if we are constantly unhappy.

Chronic unhappiness and sloth are inextricably intertwined. The slothful settle into a condition in which they feel that nothing is asked of them except to suffer; and, though they may hate the suffering, they feel it absolves them from action, from trying to bring about change. Religion becomes the 'opiate' of which Marx complained, lulling them with soothing words about the creative value of suffering when they should be taking responsibility for initiating change.

We are surprisingly bad at being happy, at selecting the paths in life which would bring us joy and fulfilment rather than the ones which bring us to pain and destruction. But, having observed this bias in ourselves, we can note that when we turn our suffering into a virtue we are steering too close to the sin of sloth. Collectively, sloth opens the way to tryanny and persecution. Individually, it turns people into tiresome miseries who have forgotten the joy of living. As always, it is worth getting wise to our own perversity.

6: Avarice

'GETTING AND SPENDING', those two exhausting enterprises, are each, it seems to me, a form of avarice. The miser holds on to what he has, preferring to live in discomfort or to see others miserable rather than touch his precious hoard. The spendthrift pours out money like water in a desperate attempt to 'get' possessions, fun or status. He is a little more attractive than the miser, but not much. Both have a cold selfishness that is indifferent to the needs of others and which quickly kills love in those who are near to them.

Both, too, have excellent alibis for the way they behave. Bunyan, in *The Holy War*, describes Satan sending Covetousness as a secret agent into the city of Mansoul. He knows better, however, than to call himself by such a name — the inhabitants would recognise and expel him at once. Instead he calls himself Mr. Prudent-Thrifty.

The Prudent-Thrifties are a large and influential clan in our society. Pick up any daily newspaper and many of the advertisements are aimed at the Prudent-Thrifties, urging them to insure and invest or to start collecting something (wine, antiques) in which they have no intrinsic interest or enjoyment but which may keep the wolf from some distant door.

Mr. Prudent-Thrifty makes investment his constant study. Mrs. Prudent-Thrifty talks of 'Which?' as if of Holy Writ, and would never make any purchase without consulting its oracle. She is already buying up huge quantities of toilet-rolls and other commodities said to be getting scarce. None of that nonsense about the lilies of the field for the Prudent-Thrifties. The lilies, after all, don't require toilet-paper, or any of the acquisitions (wine and antiques, for example) which civilised man feels are essential to his well-being.

The Spendthrifts, on the other hand, seem to live in a perpetual daze of overdrafts; Bunyan might have called them the Generous-to-a-Faults. Whatever money they have seems to dribble away like water into dry ground. Their apparent generosity is a travesty of the real thing. It is based partly on a need for immediate satisfaction and an inability to wait, partly on carelessness and *laissez faire*; above all, it comes from an unreal attitude to life, a childish attempt to retreat into irresponsibility.

Most of us dither somewhere between these two extremes, making occasional excursions into one condition or the other. Some people swing rapidly between the two; others, like Scrooge or Micawber, firmly take up one position and stay there, unless they are lucky enough to get a visit from Jacob Marley. Money, it must be admitted, is very, very difficult to live with (or without!); but, unless we dodge the whole conflict by taking a vow of poverty, then we can learn a very great deal about ourselves by seeing just what we do with the money we have.

What seems to be true for many of us is that money is intensely emotive, a potent source of fear and hope, of excitement and despair. Christ implied that it was a god whom men worshipped as an alternative to the true God; and it is as a god that men turn to it, asking for what they want in life. Scrooge asked it for power, and got it; Micawber for happiness, which was less easy for it to grant. The Prudent-Thrifties ask it for a guarantee that they will never, in sickness or in health, in youth or in age, suffer discomfort or inconvenience; and they too probably get what they ask, within limits (discomfort not being entirely under money's control.)

Money is fantastically powerful, and it is a real temptation to fall down and worship it. Probably none of us is exempt from making the surreptitious sacrifice from time to time.

And why shouldn't we? I suppose because the love of money is a deadly drink, poisoned in its dregs with fear. The avaricious man (and his counter-part) is riddled with fear. He has experienced poverty, hunger, ignominy, illness, before, and is determined that something so dreadful must not happen to him again if he can help it. The only way he can help it is to shore up the future with money, and so he saves and saves. (The spendthrift, on the other hand, grabs and grabs the things that money can buy. Above all, the avaricious man needs to feel that he is independent of others, that he need never ask anyone for help. (And, contrariwise, he is scornful of anyone who feels a need to ask *him* for help. *He* has managed; why can't they?)

The trouble is that, if you neither give nor receive help (and to be a whole person you need to do both repeatedly), then you can know nothing of love, and you are liable to become, like Scrooge, a desperately lonely person who can no longer even remember how to be happy with other people.

Christianity is about being vulnerable, and avarice is a determined attempt never to be vulnerable again. If you make yourself invulnerable (so far as the ironies of life allow), you will not end your days subsisting on the old-age pension, lying in the geriatric ward or coughing in a damp basement. On the other hand, you may have missed much of the delight of living.

> *Some folks work and slave,*
> *Some folks do, some folks do,*
> *To buy themselves a grave,*
> *But that's not me nor you.*

I hope not, anyway.

7: Anger

I GREW UP in the sort of household where there was never a row and scarcely ever a cross word (among the grown-ups, that is. My sister and I were nearer to nature). The result is that I have been morbidly fascinated ever since by people who can let their anger rip.

How *dare* they, I think, hugging myself in childish glee when I overhear two or more people going at it hammer and tongs. No doubt rows can be unpleasant for others, particularly children, but I am secretly cheering the combatants on, revelling in the honesty and openness of their feelings — so much easier to comprehend than the awful, martyred faces of those who suffer in silence. What I like about a good barney of any sort is that everyone comes down off their high horse and emerges as a normal, selfish human being instead of the saint they are pretending to be. From such moments of truth relationship can grow.

So what price anger as a sin? Anger is as natural to us as the emotion of love or fear, and quite as necessary to our self-preservation. If we could not be angry we should be the perpetual victim of others' selfishness (some people are unlucky enough to have a poor capacity for anger and do become victims). If we *can* be angry, we can use it as a sort of balancing device in our dealings with others — to tell us when we are being taken advantage of, and to put things right quickly. Being long-suffering, a habit rather excessively admired among Christians, can easily be a mask for cowardice or sloth.

Christians have sometimes got muddled, too, about normal anger, regarding the expression of it as naughty behaviour while offering no hint of how else to deal with the seething rage that lay beneath. That approach achieves little but duodenal ulcers and a damaging split between what a man feels and what he lets himself know that he feels. If he is made to feel wicked if he expresses anger or even feels it, then he learns to pretend, even to himself, that he is full of brotherly love. And Lord save us all from *that* kind of brotherly love.

It is about here, I think, that we begin to approach the sort of anger that is a sin. If a man feels he is 'too good' to feel anger, then anger, denied and repressed, works like a poison in the personality. For some it turns inward, and becomes a state of frozen depression. For others it gets turned into envy or bitterness, resentment, and hate. Flashes of wounding sarcasm, cutting asides, a determination to destroy the joy or hope of others, all emerge from this infected area like mosquitoes from a swamp. Doctors tell me that certain physical illnesses seem to them to be related to long-standing resentments — grievances which their owners have no intention of giving up, even when the cost to themselves is ruinous.

Perhaps the most destructive form of anger is the lust for revenge. A man I knew who was a prisoner in Auschwitz and whose wife died there told me that, for a couple of years after the end of the war, he could think of nothing but hatred for his captors and a desire to revenge himself and others. He could not settle anywhere, plan a career for himself or establish new human relationships, since hatred occupied him so entirely. Then one day, suddenly, it came to him that it was himself he was injuring and not the Nazis, and from that day he was able to begin life anew.

Anger, as in his case, can be more than justified, and yet there comes a point where it must be, quite simply, given up before it shatters the person who feels it. We all know the experience of going over and over some event where another person has behaved badly towards us, groaning over the smart replies we didn't make, planning letters, or telephone calls, or interviews, in which we are going to give our injurer a 'piece of our mind'.

An occasional episode of this kind is enlivening and exciting. Too many such episodes, particularly if they are always with the same person, choke us with undischarged rage. Just as bad, they drive us to interminable, ludicrous self-justification — states of mind in which we see ourselves as perfect and our attackers as impossible villains. And, if this unhappy state of affairs continues for long, we begin to move towards the paranoid state of regarding ourselves as the victims of contrived persecution. Anger must be 'let go of' (though not denied or repressed) long before we get to this stage, just so that we can get on with the more interesting business of living.

The greatest spiritual giants, like the Desert Fathers, seem to have a knack of 'letting go' of anger rather more quickly than most of us can manage. Rage sweeps through *us* in a form of possession; and, because we do not get to know the devils within us as the hermits so bravely did, we are momentarily helpless. Choice only returns when we begin to recover. What matters most, however, is that we admit the deep reservoirs of anger within us (as the Fathers repeatedly did), tempestuous floods over which we have less control than we would like but on which we can just keep afloat.

One thing more about anger — we can learn about our devils from the things that make us angry. When we feel our hearts beating, our blood pulsing and our voice beginning to tremble in argument over some issue not immediately connected with our own lives — the Third World, say, or drugs, pornography, adultery, Marxism, capitalism, women priests, or whatever it may be — we can know that something is not well within.

If there is one area in which I know my emotions are suspect, it is when I feel moral indignation.

8: Pride

THERE IS A Sufi story of a baby elephant who, because of a misunderstanding, grew up firmly believing that he was a mouse. Friends and others tried to expostulate with him; even the genuine mice occasionally tried to put in a timid word; but it was no good. He had decided in his own mind that he was a mouse, and nothing would shake his belief.

Pride works in just this way. Early in life we have settled our identity, our role, our belief, and nothing, no expostulation or objection or failure, will be allowed to interfere with it if we can help it. Provided we remain strong, we can, like the elephant, trample upon objections, our own and other people's. Secure in what Merton called a 'self-constructed identity', we can bask in the rays of our own self-congratulation.

It is, of course, hard work. Living up to a pseudo-identity involves us in doing many things we don't really want to do. (No doubt the elephant found himself obliged to eat cheese and look as if he liked it.) It can involve us in exhausting routines of cleaning, tidying-up and cooking — if the pseudo-identity is that of a good housewife; in highbrow tastes that don't really appeal to us, if the pseudo-identity is that of an intellectual; of assiduous church-going, if it is that of a good Christian; of ambitious educational schemes for our children, if their success feeds our identity. Pride is not interested in inner satisfaction; all it requires is that we strive to keep our rosy dream of ourselves and our families intact, and that we try to make others believe in it too.

The tragedy of pride is that it cuts people off from one another; other people soon become a threat to a fragile identity. We are obliged to repudiate other people, as the elephant felt obliged to repudiate the real mice, to feel superior to them, to tell ourselves how much better *we* manage things. We have to pretend not to hear when they come out with some statement about themselves which exposes us for the shams that we are. We dare not share our suffering with them.

And, for all our belief of what a help we are to others (a favourite dream of the proud), we cannot respond very accurately to their needs and demands, since everything must be referred to the idol we really worship — the stereotype, or identity, with which we are desperately trying to conform. Yet such is our longing for identity, to be Somebody for other people, that turning our back on this idol is the hardest thing we ever have to do.

The Christian religion, like all great religions, tells us that life for a man consists of refusing this intolerably seductive idol, and turning instead to the true God in whom a mysterious and unimaginable identity is to be found. The Bible is wise about the conditions in which men often do make this costly inner journey, noting that in illness, bereavement, poverty, failure, disgrace, many of us at last do find the courage to rip off the idiot mask of our pseudo-identity and discover that there is another, more human, face beneath it. Yet we do not have to wait for catastrophe. We can learn the lesson from others, or we can, if we are humorous and lighthearted enough, stumble upon it for ourselves.

What is so terrible about pride, however, is that it winkles its deadly way into the very therapy that is supposed to cure us. The Christian religion, with its magnificent insights into the way in which a man may liberate himself from idols and worship God, itself becomes a stereotype to which we desperately cling, feeling that anything is better than the unknown. In fact it offers us a whole wardrobe of pseudo-identities. Some of them are intellectual, doctrinal, dogmatic or confessional identities, and they are bad enough; but there are worse, if only because the pride in them is harder to detect.

There are, for instance, the identities of 'the saint', 'the good man or woman', 'the good Christian'. There is 'helping others'. There is 'setting a good example'. There is 'upholding standards', 'taking a stand' and many more. These masks are terribly attractive to us, but hidden behind them is the pitiful truth: we are no more than human. It is *we* who need help, *we* who are the 'weaker brethren', *we* who are 'the poor'; and though we wriggle and struggle at the knowledge and long to find ourselves in some grander, more heroic role, so long as we do so we are living in our self-constructed identity and have not really begun our journey at all.

We are not saints and we are not good, except like you-know-who's egg, in parts. If we can, on occasion, help others, it is only a matter of time before we need every bit as much help in return. The beginning of wisdom, not to mention the fear of the Lord, is finally to face this unwelcome, indissoluble fact about ourselves — that we are human — and find that it does not overcome us, that on the contrary it fills us with laughter. A writer was complaining recently in a Christian magazine that jokes were sometimes made about Christianity on television, just as if we were not funny, or were somehow sacrosanct.

The more they laugh at us, the better. The more *we* laugh at us, the better. How else are we to counter our inflationary tendencies, our solemnity, our longing to find ourselves holy or special or good?

There is an Hasidic story of a pious Jew complaining to a holy man and saying: 'I have laboured hard and long in the service of the Lord, and yet I have received no improvement. I am still an ordinary and ignorant person.' 'Ah!' said the Baalshem, 'but you have gained the realisation that you are ordinary and ignorant.'

I bet the Jew wasn't a bit grateful.

III

SEVEN CHRISTIAN WORDS

1: Conversion

I AM ONE of those who have had what is called a 'conversion experience'. Sitting on a seat in a London park at the age of twenty I had a shattering vision of joy and goodness, and went away aghast at what had happened to me. It was months before I could start to digest the strangeness of it, years before I could think coolly about it.

The most difficult and dangerous thing about such an experience, it strikes me in retrospect, is the feeling of specialness it creates. The recipient feels that something unique has happened to him, and that therefore he has some particular message for others. He may not be lucky, though I was, in finding those who can help him disentangle whatever is real and true about the conversion from his paranoia or from his feelings of omnipotence. But, in any case, it will take him many years to discover the peculiar paradox of specialness: that it is everyone's birthright, and so it is to be found finally in ordinariness.

I am not sneering at the conversion experience, which for so many has been a sort of key moment of life, but I sometimes wonder uneasily at the importance Christianity has given to it. When I speculate about why some people have it and others don't, I find myself inclining to the view that it comes to those who have a particularly strong need for affirmation, who need, transiently at least, to discover their own specialness.

In discovering their specialness they simultaneously discover God. Or, rather, the opposite. They discover God, and this affirms their own uniqueness.

A recent speaker on a B.B.C. television programme, asked

what he felt was required to have this kind of knock-out experience of God, said 'desperation', and this strikes me as a profound truth. The limitation of the self, and the inescapable knowledge of the limitation, becomes, for some people, such an acute form of suffering that something else has to happen; and what happens is conversion.

I had got this far once in a discussion about conversion when someone said indignantly, 'But what about the Holy Spirit?' We were back to what seems a very old-fashioned *deus ex machina* view of the Holy Spirit, rushing on to the scene to give recalcitrant, or specially chosen, recipients a nudge.

I don't think such a view of the Holy Spirit or of conversion really stands up to our modern understanding of man. It seems unlikely that God has favourites, or that he needs to be manipulative in such a way. It is really a man's whole life which is his conversion, or non-conversion, experience; and how far he gets in the movement towards love may depend as much upon others as it depends upon his conscious choice.

More and more I incline to the view of the French writer Hubert Benoit that all men, however mistakenly or blindly, work inwardly for liberation. 'All men work, whether they know it or not, to overcome their fundamental lack . . . All that man does is aimed at compensating a fundamental disharmony.' But perhaps 'all men' can only know what they do when claims to 'chosenness' and 'specialness' are everywhere surrendered.

2: Sacrament

THERE ARE CERTAIN words that I always hope non-believing friends won't ask me to explain to them, and one of them is 'sacrament'. Since I know what the word means it is not my own ignorance that I fear to find exposed, but rather a more fundamental difficulty I have about the whole idea.

Most people, Christian or not, are ready enough to admit that there have been in their lives moments of such rare luminosity that it was easy to believe, if not in God, at least in a spiritual purpose working through the common events of life. For me some of those moments, and some of the most important of them, have come by way of Christianity — the conversion experience itself, and a number of other times in prayer or at the Mass. Many other such moments in my life have not taken this route at all, but have come by aesthetic experience, sexual experience, childbirth, friendship.

Perhaps I am wrong — I'd like to be wrong about it — but I have a feeling that, whatever we say about the incarnational nature of Christianity, we are reluctant to admit that *that* sort of experience is as worthwhile, or genuine, or satisfactory, spiritually speaking, as those which come to us in a more directly spiritual form. There is still a Puritan unwillingness — and I feel it strongly in myself — to admit that sexuality, for example, even between a couple who love each other deeply, can be as spiritually meaningful to them as the Holy Communion.

What therefore makes me uneasy about 'sacraments' is the uncertainty of whether we, as Christians, believe that there are two kinds of sacrament or only one kind of sacrament. Given that there can be a sort of 'holy moment' which exists independently of the sacraments prescribed by the Church, do we say that that isn't what *we* mean by a sacrament? Or that there are, as it were, 'godly' sacraments and 'human' sacraments?

For what seems to happen in practice is that, wherever we most deeply enter into our humanity, in all its weakness, helplessness, vulnerability to others, then there, most certainly, do we seem to find God; sometimes at appalling cost, but no matter, we find him. And, as I get older, I find it more and more difficult to mind about *where* this happens, and in what circumstances. I am so grateful that it happens at all. To be truly human we have to learn, patiently and humbly, to admit our terrible indigence — the saints were good at this: and, if we ever get to that point, then we may become as thrifty as sparrows, gratefully pecking up divine love wherever we can find it.

This is not to decry the formal sacraments: it is a great blessing that they can be offered to us at regular times, like meals from a soup kitchen for the starving. Only the banquet of life goes on too, simultaneously, and there is no need to be so quixotic as to refuse our invitation or to deny the goodness of the fare.

3: Poverty

ONE OF THE MOST interesting (and terrifying) aspects of Christianity is its enthusiasm for poverty. Most of us find our method for shuffling off this uncomfortable 'blessing' which our religion bestows on us, like an eccentric fairy godmother who has got her spells mixed.

Some, perhaps the least hypocritical, simply decide that poverty doesn't mean them, and, like Roy Thomson in a famous television broadcast, can see no reason why the rich should not get into the kingdom of heaven. Some really are generous with what they have. Some are poor with such ostentation that they are as good as con men at getting a fiver off their fellow-Christians. Some, as in religious communities, are poor with an absolute security that is the envy of the rest of us, always wondering where the money for the rates or the electricity bill is coming from. Some are poorish (this applies to many of the clergy), hoping to make up to their children (and themselves) for what they miss by quality of living; and, on the whole, this is one of the more dignified stances a Christian can take.

But it is clear that it takes all sorts to make a kingdom; and comic creatures that we are, like the rogues who abound in the parables, we scheme and manipulate, dreading the freedom that is prepared for us.

I cannot pretend to have got very far in unmasking my own pretensions about money, but I have made one small discovery about poverty now. If it is true that 'time is money' in the sense that time used up makes money, then, if you renounce money, at least to some extent, what you have is unused-up time. The more keen you are on making money, or on acquiring the sort of fame and success which lead to making money, then the less free, the less enjoyable, your life becomes. The factory-worker who works all weekend to get his overtime, or the tycoon who cannot take a holiday and is all set for his coronary, have this in common, that they are deprived of a birthright as natural as sun or air, that of free time.

Freedom of every sort seems to be inextricably mixed with poverty, or what I would sooner call medium poverty. (Really abysmal poverty seems to lead to stereotyped behaviour as much as fantastic riches.) This, I think, is not because it matters in itself to have a bit of money or success, but because we so easily forget our insecurity; and, once we forget it, we behave like monsters to one another. But, given the open wound of never enough money, it becomes harder to forget, though other wounds do as well — illness, or physical handicaps, or simply the humiliation of our own personality.

And, given an omnipresent insecurity, the bitter sense of

slavery, we are as ready as the children of Israel to get up and go at the moment life calls us in search of freedom. If we expect insecurity, then that at once is a sort of freedom, allowing us to do and say things which need doing and saying but which may be socially risky. We belong to no Establishment, need swallow no propaganda, can afford to look all authority coolly in the eye. It seems a small price to pay.

4: Clergy

'I LIKE WICKERS,' my four-year-old daughter once observed as we passed a strange clergyman in the street; and I knew how she felt, having always had a soft spot for them myself. I grew up in an unchurchy household in which one of my parents had a strong antipathy to the clergy; but, far from putting me off, this only made them seem the more intriguing. And then, when I was nine or so, I became friendly with a local curate, and my good opinion was confirmed.

It was therefore a great shock a few years later to discover that the clergy had, traditionally, a very different image from the warm and lively one I had made for them. Victorian literature, and even more Edwardian literature, abounded in unpleasant clergymen — hypocrites, floggers, silly asses, men with plums in their mouths (this tradition still survives on the stage, though it grows weaker), or worst of all, men like the schoolmaster-clergyman in Forster's *The Longest Journey* who are cold, narrow, insensitive and life-denying.

What has only gradually occurred to me is that the loathing of Victorian and Edwardian writers, and indeed the behaviour of some of the clergy who were their models, sprang from the fact that the clergy were then very much part of the power structure. In the country they were part of the squirearchy — which, judging by books like *Akenfield*, was a much more terrible instrument of oppression than we have sentimentally believed. In the towns they were very much part of the establishment; and even the best of them, even the ones who cared terribly about social injustice, were men from a different culture who spoke with a different accent.

But that has all gone, had already gone by the time I was born; and, with the clear eyes of a child, I knew that the local clergy did not represent temporal power. I saw them as rare, slightly exotic birds in a rather dull suburban setting, dressing up in strange clothes, busy or free in quite a different rhythm from everyone else, friendly, concerned, real.

It is only as an adult that I can begin to count the cost (and the gain) of that loss of power, to know the psychological pain of being 'different' and the impotence of losing a social role. What role has the clergyman now that his old temporal power has been ripped from him like a carpet from under his feet? A role that I do not envy, though I value it more than I can say, which is perhaps analogous to that of the poet or the artist, a man who not only points to meaning but whose life *is* the meaning.

In the West we tend to think of poets as rather earnest people, but what I have in mind is more the sort of poet/artist/sage who drifts through Zen and other Oriental writing, bringing a kind of lightness and irony to what must have been a fairly rigid society, walking lightly, extraordinary among the ordinary, and ordinary among the extraordinary.

'My miracle,' remarked one of them, 'is that when I feel hungry I eat, and when I feel thirsty I drink.' I would like to present that, in letters of gold (if that were not too affected for Zen), to every seminarian in the country.

5: Confession

IT USED TO irritate a friend of mine that, when he went to confession, he never got the chance to tell the priest the good things he had done.

Sacramental confession stands on a narrow base. It limits itself, as a surgeon limits himself in an operation, to one small section which, isolated from the rest, can look strangely inhuman. There have been times in my life when I have valued this clinical kind of confession as a kind of antisepsis of the spirit. I also came, over a period of time, to value the awareness it gave me that my life followed a seemingly inevitable pattern. I always committed the same sins, never any new ones — I got neither better nor worse; the disease was chronic.

Once I had made this discovery, however, the practice gradually became for me emptier. Enlightened priests expanded the old form of confession into a general chat about what I was up to (as has, I believe, become general practice); and, though they were as sensitive and intelligent as I could wish, this did not seem to help particularly.

It was partly that I no longer felt able to examine or talk about myself in such an exclusive atmosphere of sin, nor did I necessarily want to do it with clergy. What makes me, and most people I know, most guilty is not their sins, either of omission or commission, but their fantasies. It is often a relief to be able to confide our darker fantasies to others, but we cannot do so by an act of will; or at least this is a brutal method. We can do it best with those we love, those who know us profoundly and know what weight to give to the matter, and at moments which flow naturally from intimate conversation.

So that my dilemma over confession is simply this — to include such fantasies feels inappropriate and, to me, psychologically damaging; to omit them falsifies the picture.

And in any case, however guilty such fantasies can make me

feel, I do not regard them as 'sin.' The guilt seems to me ir-
rational, stemming, as it does with everyone, from painful early
experiences which were by no stretch of imagination my
fault.

Sin strikes me as a very different matter; not the rather
fiddling obsession with envy and anger and small untruths that
we often make it out to be, but something much more terrible — a determined, obstinate choice of unreality and self-
deception which has become a whole life-style. For the most
part we are as unaware of it as we are unaware of our own
appearance seen from the back view, too unaware to confess it.
It is only when we catch a sudden glimpse of our own unreality
through the distortions it may produce in our children, our
marriage partners, or others who are close, that awareness
breaks through.

I suppose that is the moment for sacramental confession — an act to hold the door ajar for a moment or two so
that we may see before we gratefully return to oblivion. It is
almost impersonal; in fact I wonder if we should not talk of
being 'sinned through' as Buddhists talk of being 'breathed
through'.

6: Fellowship

I HAVE NEVER quite understood the expression 'the Body of
Christ' as applied to the unity of Christians within their
parishes, confessions, or the world-wide Church, which is to say
that I do not think it is something I have fully experienced.
The fellowship aspect of Christianity, I can say without any
hesitation at all, has been the one that I have found most
difficult.

I used to think it was intellectual snobbery that made it so
difficult for me to enjoy the social life of the parish, but looking

back over the years I think it had far more to do with the rigidity of male/female roles. In the first parish where I really tried to be a practising Christian the two sexes went, quite naturally and unselfconsciously, their separate ways. The women met to talk about 'feminine' topics, they were always responsible for providing nourishment at parish meetings, they arranged flowers. The men busied themselves with the more important matters. I am not a natural sandwich-cutter and flower-arranger, and it made for a sense of loneliness and oddness for which I compensated by finding more congenial Christian friends outside the parish.

Nowadays, however, a vast change has begun to work in the Church. Women really do feel much more equal — hence the urgency of the ordination issue — and people in general are much more demanding (rightly so) about the need for groups of any kind to be effective. We long for better, deeper, relationships with other human beings, and are more impatient of falsity and empty phrases.

One way in which the old claustrophobia is overcome is in new outward-looking groups, more concerned about the social needs of the parish than with the internal matters. In the suburban parish where I used to live, such a group, composed equally of men and women, was very effective in sponsoring public meetings about world hunger and the population explosion, and in fighting a battle to get the physically disabled more integrated into the community. And such efforts at pricking the social conscience are widespread.

All the same, I hope the 'helping' aspect of Christianity will not carry us away entirely. 'Helping' makes it so appallingly easy to overlook how much help we ourselves need if we are to get any glimmer of wholeness. As any parish priest knows, his parishioners carry their full share of marital and family problems, of mental and physical illness, of financial and other fears. Yet, with the exception of physical illness which alone is not seen as a 'failure' (perhaps it should be, at least as much or as little as the others), how few of these private agonies are shared in any degree within 'the Christian family.' For the most part, we are not close enough to one another to get 'found out' (in the way that people are in religious communities, for example) and we have not enough trust, as yet, voluntarily to share. This seems to me to be one of the areas where Christian practice must undergo a revolution if it is to recover enough vitality to attract others.

7: Suffering

'There is also a cup of pain for you to drink all up
Or setting it aside for sweeter drink
Thirst ever more,'

says Stevie Smith in her poem, 'And so to fatness come'; and she is outlining what for me is the core of all religious approaches to life. Through suffering we come to life and liberty.

But what kind of suffering? The interesting thing is that, for different generations, the suffering is different; and this is not just because outward conditions change, so that some men had to wrestle with the Plague in the light of their beliefs and others with the horrors of the trenches. It is rather that consciousness itself changes, so that what for one generation is unchangeable fact, like feudalism or the subservience of women, is for another the grinding machine in which the diamond is polished.

The true asceticism is to discover what suffering is right for us, which cup of grief we must drink right up. (So afraid are we of freedom that we would sooner drink the wrong potion, however bitter. Self-destructive creatures that we are, we don't easily choose life.)

I suggest that for us the cup of grief is the cup of

consciousness. 'I am glad I grew up in the old days before people knew anything about sex,' an elderly relative said to me the other day. In the old days you could dodge the grief of consciousness not only of sex but of all the major passions. You did not have to enter that lonely inner landscape and discover murderous hate and jealousy, longings to dominate and manipulate or to be helplessly dependent, fears and suspicions of your fellow-men, or attempts to control them through illness. You could be a nice person — one rather like Newman's gentleman who did not inflict pain.

In the old days, did I say? But we do it still. We strive to suppress through censorship anything that reminds us of those fearful inner-demons, and we resist fiercely the truths that our nearest and dearest try to show us. It's not hard to see why. The shame of self-discovery reduces us to infancy — we are four years old and have been caught stealing the jam again — and the centuries of talk about repentance don't make the experience a whit easier.

And yet . . . we want to be caught; we know that, if we do not drink the cup of grief, we will thirst for evermore, and never come to fatness at all. And it's not just that we thirst, but that we create a desert around us. Newman's gentleman, whether he likes it or not, inflicts pain through refusing to admit the pain within. His self-deception, evident in every word and gesture, forces all about him to acts of falsity; whatever game we play, our relatives and friends and colleagues are forced to join the team, willy-nilly.

But Christians do know, at least theoretically, that we are *not* 'nice people', and that repentance is our only hope. And a Christian writer like Bunyan, who made most of his villains gentlemen and ladies, knew that 'the World' was a lying and murderous place. We cannot however, adopt the sectarian solution of projecting all badness outwards on to others and believing that we, and our group, are saved. That way paranoia lies. Nor can we adopt the alternative path of assuming that everyone is quite nice really, because it is so demonstrably untrue.

We are left with the third choice, the 'cup of grief that we must drink right up', of discovering that badness, no more and no less than good, lies within us. Like the Kingdom of Heaven.

IV

PRAYER AND PRE-PRAYER

1: What Do You Mean, Prayer?

UNTIL A FEW years ago it was simply taken for granted that prayer was something that churchgoing people 'did'. As an adolescent I remember feeling an intense curiosity about what was going on when someone knelt down, closed their eyes, and kept more or less still.

It seemed, for a start, such an unlikely position in which to do any of the sort of things that I was told prayer was about. If you were talking to God, it seemed a strange pose for a chat. If you were listening to God, the same. One would not, after all, conduct a telephone conversation on the floor, kneeling, with one's eyes closed. Yet again, this was God, who was (I reasoned) somewhat grander than the Queen; and most people did not idly chat to royalty while lying in bed or prostrate on the sofa.

This first conundrum about prayer really reached the heart of all subsequent problems. There was for me something affected and self-conscious about prayer as deeply rooted as, but more damaging than, my snobbery about royalty. It was not something I could do naturally.

Yet the clergy went on exhorting me and others to pray, and those little pious books told me to do it as part of a 'rule of life' — clearly assuming that it was something any fool could do. C. S. Lewis, making a perilous short-cut around the difficulty, thought it was simply a matter of will-power. Anyone, after all, could recite words out of books.

And, above all, there were lots of people, in church, their faces buried in their hands, presumably doing something and not just daydreaming, as I was. (As I have grown older, I have entertained the nasty suspicion that most people are neither much better nor worse than I am, but in those days I was easily awed.) What went on in their heads? Murmured ejaculations — I believe 'arrow prayers' was what people liked to call them — peaceful, trance-like states, long one-sided conversations with God, like that of Betjeman's dowager?

And what of liturgical prayer? What did people think about during those long stretches of psalms? Did they dutifully think themselves naughty during the more penitent passages of the Mass, and then try to work themselves into an appropriate mood of reverence in order to receive Communion? Or were they worrying about money, their marital problems, and the general anguish of being human?

In subsequent articles I hope to go into the question of what prayer (using the word pretty widely) may mean to a twentieth-century person; but, for the moment, I just want to remind myself of what was so wrong about my adolescent struggles with the subject, partly as a result of poor teaching, partly because of the peculiarities of my own temperament.

One basic mistake was that I took it all so seriously and did not realise that prayer, like so much that is precious to human beings, is at bottom a comic thing to do. Given the incongruity between God and man, between timelessness and time, a man at prayer is a funny sight.

I wish that I had seen this earlier, as I also wish that I had seen that it mattered very little that what most people were doing in church (as in private prayer) was woolgathering. In youth I despised woolgathering; it is only as I grow older that I begin to see it as a lovely and distinctively human activity, one of which by no means everyone is capable.

2: Letting the Mind Run Down

WHEN I REMARKED once at a public discussion about prayer that I thought just sitting and woolgathering was a useful exercise, a nun in the audience remarked sharply: 'But that's just wasting time!' I felt rather deflated and at odd moments ever since have thought of replies I might have made but didn't.

What I should certainly have made clearer than I did was that I did not really suppose that sitting and woolgathering was prayer, except in some very rudimentary form, but rather that it was something you might call 'pre-prayer'. I don't think, amateurs at prayer as most of us are, that we pay half enough attention to pre-prayer. Like all amateurs we see the romance but not the pitfalls, the fears and the costly self-giving. We have the audacity to suppose that prayer is something we ought to be able to do.

In most cases I don't believe it is something we can do, not because we lack some sort of talent or goodness, but because we are simply too strung up by the stresses of everyday life. If prayer is, as I believe, not a matter of uttering a few words, even if deeply felt, but of achieving a certain sort of creative *awareness*, then it is idle to suppose that this can be fitted in, like physical jerks, between dressing and eating breakfast.

Mentally, emotionally, we are not ready for anything you could begin to call prayer. We have been bred, by a dozen different social pressures, to tremendous activity; and, when the activity ceases, we fall, not surprisingly, into extreme fatigue; both these states are inimical to prayer.

Occasionally — recuperating from illness, on holiday, inspired by aesthetic experience — we stumble into the precious awareness. Or we may choose deliberately to cultivate it by denying ourselves so much activity, though this can be a costly choice in our society. But in the main we are too desperately busy, not necessarily through any fault of our own, to achieve prayer.

What ought to be our concern, and what is, in any case, an absolutely necessary first step, is pre-prayer, the process of letting the mind run down, like a clock, to a state of stillness. What we need, wrote Merton in *Conjectures of a Guilty Bystander*, is 'to trifle and vegetate without feeling guilty about it'. He was already a hermit by the time he wrote that, and one might suppose he would need pre-prayer rather less than some of us do; but he seemed to feel that trifling and vegetating, i.e. 'just wasting time', was a precious function and certainly one without which useful activity was impossible.

Sloth, with its underlying fear of action, is not the danger which bedevils us nowadays; busyness is.

3: Towards Stillness

THOSE OF US who have to combine our attempts at prayer with strenuous family and professional activities, have to begin with pre-prayer.

Even when we have learned how inimical excessive fatigue can be to prayer and trained ourselves to avoid it rather as a good surgeon avoids late nights, there are times when we are just too tired, agitated, nervous and overwrought to compose ourselves very successfully. In such a condition even to sit still for half-an-hour can become torture — we may feel a compulsion to move about, to talk to other people, to engage in energetic work.

In this condition stillness, and the accompanying awareness that makes prayer so precious to us, is not a quickly realisable state; it is only something we can work towards, rather than away from, like the light at the end of a tunnel. In our disintegrated state it is sometimes difficult even to *want* to move back towards stillness, and it is here, perhaps, that obedience comes in — the kind of obedience that makes a formal, or informal, retreat from time to time, the kind that refuses invitations, the kind that can say no to the many apparently harmless seductions of life which eat up our energy and keep us continually distracted.

But, in the running down process towards stillness, pre-prayer seems to me to be a necessity. To begin with, it often consists of almost prising ourselves by force out of our compulsive working in order to clear an inner space in which something else can happen. This is, it seems to me, a painful process (which is why compulsive workers tend not to attempt it), since at first glance the inner space seems terrifyingly arid.

A filling up of the space with the right kind of nonsense helps a bit until we can bear it — rather in the way Wittgenstein used to interpose his mind-breaking bouts of thinking with watching Betty Hutton films. Fierce gardening helps *me*, I think because aggression is one of the things that comes between me and stillness, but then it is for many people.

Art sometimes works faster than almost anything, if we are lucky in coming across the right thing at the right moment; I remember coming out of a sculpture exhibition at the Tate feeling as if I had been bathed in balm. Solitude also helps me — I feel myself growing and expanding in it, rather as if I were discovering I could use limbs that had become atrophied — but people vary a lot about this. Looking after oneself physically — getting enough sleep, eating good food, living more slowly — are all part of pre-prayer.

The movement from pre-prayer to prayer is an imperceptible one, but somewhere along that road we find to our delight that we can sit still, that we can *be* still, and that life and people cease to be an intolerable demand. We know ourselves again as part of a landscape.

4: Deepening Awareness

THE MORE I struggle with the idea of prayer, the more I discover that what I am really after is a deepened awareness. Awareness of what? The pat answer is, of course, God; but, if I only succeeded in becoming more aware of the natural world, of other people, of the world of movement within my own body, I should feel that I had come to know more about God.

How is this awareness attained? It is here, I think, that one of the great divides between different groups of Christians occurs — the kind where it is really very difficult to hear what the others are saying and to recognise that their integrity is no less than one's own.

One group conceives of prayer as a regular discipline, a daily or nightly exercise. It believes in the use of words from books and in continuing with the exercise no matter how arid and painful it becomes; it thinks that, if this is not practised, then the result is a slipping away from God and the awareness of God.

The other group claims to find this 'discipline' of prayer an impossibility; members of it may refuse to use prayers that need words, and to prefer 'sitting' in silence. They would claim that their whole life is their prayer (as, of course, the first group would probably claim too). Obviously they are open to charges of laziness from the first group, but they would probably simply shrug their shoulders cheerfully and say: 'O.K., we're lazy!'

We know little as yet about the psychology of prayer, but what I suspect we may be dealing with is people who attain awareness through a concentration, a 'sharpening' of their faculties and those who do so through relaxing concentration, through a 'diffusing' of their faculties.

The first group do best by fixing their minds in a particular way, the second by letting their minds run free. Since I come squarely in the second group, I know that for me prayer is, as it were, something seen out of the corner of the eye. When I am writing, or reading, or cooking, or watching television, or talking to friends and family, I am slipping in and out of the awareness that is precious to me. When I try to 'pray' deliberately, it is gone.

But, just as the first group feels that the effectiveness of *its* kind of prayer is conditional upon its regularity, then the second group, at least in my experience, have to obey a no less stringent condition. It is to refuse to overwork and instead to try to discover the natural rhythm in life, since only a certain obedience to this makes deep awareness possible. And the penalties for this in our production-minded society can be rather formidable.

5: Space for Prayer

IF PRAYER IS something important to us, then much more of our time will be directed to trying to bring about possible conditions for prayer than to actually doing it.

I have several times compared the act of prayer with the act of writing, and here once again the comparison holds true. As a writer I seem to devote an awful lot of effort and time to clearing a space in which to write. It means turning down invitations to things like coffee mornings and conferences. It means trying to persuade my friends not to telephone me in the mornings. It means finding someone to do the housework that I can't get done.

It means, on a more seductive level, refusing jobs, and

friendships, and good works, and hobbies, that simply would not leave enough time and energy over. I'm not very good at this, because I like money and people and experimenting with doing new things (not necessarily in that order); but at bottom I know that, if I am to do what I *really* want to do, then what I have to resist is seduction — usually seduction by good causes.

Prayer seems to me to work in much the same way. We want the space in which to deepen our awareness of ourselves and of God by one method or another; but, much as we want it (almost, I sometimes think, *because* we want it so badly), we can still be tempted into activities which exhaust us and leave us as unsatisfied as ever. These may not necessarily be what people used to call 'frivolous' activities — frivolity can often feed us in unexpected ways. In fact for many Christians now it often seems to be the sheer weight of earnest and worthy duties which makes self-discovery no more than a wistful hope.

Not long ago, I got a letter from the wife of a vicar who felt totally submerged by all the duties of the parish. She felt she could not possibly opt out, even for a year or so, without hurting her husband, laying a heavier burden on him, and scandalising the parish; yet she was so sick of everything that church services had become totally meaningless to her and she was increasingly doubtful of the faith she held.

Perhaps if, collectively, we had a bit more spiritual insight, we should know that there are occasions in people's lives when a kind of moratorium on works, even good works, is what is needed most, and that this is as much a proof of their love for mankind as feeding the hungry. I guess that this is where Eastern religions have an awful lot to teach us.

6: Waiting for God

WHEN WE ARE still enough to embark on something that may be called prayer, then it seems to me that we know it by knowing ourselves part of a landscape — we feel that our sufferings are worse than other people's, our claims on life are more important than theirs, and life itself seems to impinge uncomfortably upon us.

But in stillness we are part of a whole — we can see our own life, sufferings, death, with a certain detachment and can momentarily glimpse the I-ness of others. Our ego is embarking on the transformation which is, paradoxically, at once its crucifixion and its liberation.

But, what, within this great clearing of stillness, do we actually do? At a recent gathering of people interested in prayer that I attended I noticed that people tended to talk in two quite opposite ways.

One group saw prayer largely as a *filling* of the silence, almost as one might place furniture in an empty house. For them the silence was busy with acts of love towards God and towards others, with movements and thoughts, with silent 'speaking' and listening, and with colourful imagery.

The other group seemed to want the habitation of prayer to be as bare as possible, to be a place of *not* speaking, *not* imagining, *not* forming concepts, not even listening in the usually accepted sense of the term. Waiting might be the best word for what they were doing, except that even that implies a sort of Godot-like expectancy which does them less than justice. The love for those who try to pray like this is not expressed through utterances to God, but simply in the action of sitting — like Thomas Merton's solitaries, who 'sit in the cell for the Name of God', the emphasis being on the sitting and the continuing to sit.

I suppose that most people who try to pray come somewhere between these two extremes; and within the Christian tradition there seems ample room for all of them, as well as shining examples of men and women who have prayed by each of these methods. Gradually we learn to make room for others alongside us in the landscape: others whose flowers and whose growth may be spectacularly different from our own.

7: Respecting Bodily Needs

A RECENT STUDY of obesity suggested that fat people were those who had, on the simplest sort of level, lost touch with their inner needs. Whereas normal people felt contractions of hunger in their stomach and decided it was time to eat, the very fat did not wait for these signals. The 'cue' to eat was, for them, the sight of food; and, when they saw food, they wanted to eat, and often could not stop until they had finished it all up.

I have enough of an eating problem myself to know just how difficult it is to learn to wait for inner needs to make themselves known — in fact to know that what is needed is a whole re-education of the body.

For Christians it is a particularly humbling process learning to listen to their own bodies. We have, almost without knowing it, inherited the tragic suspicion of the body that so distorted mediaeval Christianity; and many Christian statements to this day carry the implicit suggestion that, if we listen to the hints of our bodies, we shall be led into destruction. I suppose there may be people for whom this is true; but, the more I examine my own life, the more I think I made my worse mistakes by *not* listening to my body and trying to live as a sort of disembodied mind.

If Christians really listened to their bodies and tried to respect the natural rhythms within them, they could not, for a start, subscribe to the addiction to overwork. Overwork must be one of the worst spiritual dangers there is: potentially as damaging to the personality and its relationships as alcohol or drugs (it is, of course, a sort of drug). Yet the self-punishing aspects of religion have fastened upon it and turned it into a virtue.

But it isn't. A readiness to work hard and well is a good and necessary thing. But, when an individual can no longer allow himself daily or weekly leisure, holidays, adequate time in which to recuperate after illness, then, like the fat man or the alcoholic, he has reached the pathological state in which the sense of true measure has been lost.

It is no joke for any of us to try to find our way back from these states. The very real anxiety which drives us away from our natural rhythms (often disturbing, in the process, sexual and digestive functions which in turn create greater anxiety) tends to push us into excess, instead of forcing us to stop and make the humbling attempt to rediscover ourselves.

Yet, if we care about God, if we care about prayer, if we care about love, then this process of rediscovering what it means to be a man may be the very best thing we can do for the world. We may never quite get there (do we ever really overcome our worst weaknesses? I never seem to), but we cannot try without gaining a deep knowledge of humanity.

8: Prayer of Petition

I NEVER PRAY with greater intensity than when I think I am going to miss a train — a form of suffering which occurs to me frequently.

There seem to be two schools of thought about petitionary prayer. One, which is a sub-department of the 'We are all little children before our heavenly Father and should behave as such' group, is all for even the silliest petitions. The other cautions a certain discretion in what we ask for — partly, perhaps, for the very good reason that petitionary prayer has a high failure rate. (I have noticed, for instance, that I never do catch the trains that I pray to catch; and it would, in fact, take a miracle to get me aboard them, since I never start on time.)

The cruel disappointment that is created by too facile an approach to petitionary prayer is beautifully illustrated in Somerset Maugham's *Of Human Bondage*, where a child prays in perfect faith for the removal of his club foot. The glib Christian answer, 'God can say no,' does nothing to meet the human suffering involved.

On the other hand, I doubt whether I shall ever stop praying to catch trains which I am, inevitably, going to miss; and it occurs to me that, when I do so, I am giving voice to a much greater distress than that of missed appointments and irritated friends. I am perhaps expressing the fundamental quarrel each of us has with God — why did I have to be *this* kind of a person, caught for ever in the same exasperating set of personality patterns?

Like Maugham's little boy I am beating at the bounds of reality, the personal prison in which each of us finds ourselves; and for me, as for him, it is a painful matter of finding a different answer from the instinctive one of simple escape.

The person who has taught me most about petitionary prayer was a man who did not think he had any religious belief at all.

Did he never pray? I asked him once — curious as to how anyone could get by, particularly as a traveller on British Rail, without constant commerce with God. No, he never prayed to catch trains. Did he pray when he was ill? No, he had been rushed off to hospital not long before with a dangerous illness, but it had not occurred to him to pray. Did he pray for people he loved? No, he didn't pray for people he loved.

One thing, though, he said, after thinking it over, though you couldn't really call it prayer, was that, when he was up against it, in some way he found himself asking for strength just to carry on. Asking? Asking whom? He didn't know whom; he just asked.

This seemed to me to be the kind of generic petitionary prayer from which all our trivial requests are derived. To return to the child/father image: we ask for favours, as children ask for sweets and toys, when at bottom what we need is assurance that we are cared for and sustained.

9: Prayer of Intercession

SOME OF THE fundamental difficulties about the Christian faith have a way of being expressed by simple people (the sophisticates scorn to mention them) in ways that are hard to answer or forget.

I remember hearing someone describe her problem with intercessory prayer. She had got together a long, and growing, list of names, and, being of a somewhat obsessional character, could never make up her mind to leave anyone off it, as this seemed mean and ungenerous. What was meant, and had begun, as a loving act had gradually turned into a pathological exercise like going back to see if the gas is switched off when you know perfectly well that it is.

When one gets to that kind of problem in prayer, then the answer seems to be to return both to a more humorous and to a more spontaneous idea of what one is up to.

Intercession, of all kinds of prayer, needs a certain lightness of touch, a certain perspective. The built-in difficulty about it is that, being the sort of creatures we are, we can easily find ourselves wanting to control other people, or telling God what would be best for them.

Edmund Gosse, in *Father and Son*, has an amusing instance of his father praying in his hearing (he was about thirteen at the time) that he would have the grace to refuse an invitation to a party where there were to be 'theatricals'; and, to his son's fury, 'he did not scruple to remind the Deity of various objections to a life of pleasure and of the snakes that lie hidden in the grass of evening parties'.

We don't go in for that sort of prayer — we pray for the sick, the hungry, the imprisoned, the unhappy, and it often seems that the right outcome is obvious. Yet, the longer we go on in life, the more we realise how complex and ambiguous human suffering is, and how little we know of what is the right solution for others.

I daren't myself go in for lists of people to pray for, for much the same reason as the lady mentioned at the beginning of this article; and I like power too much to dare to give God advice. Yet, when I stumble across people in obvious distress — either people I know, or people who appear on television and in the newspapers — I feel, as I imagine most people do, a need to acknowledge our common humanity; to enter, even if callously briefly, their situation. I cannot spare them *enormous* amounts of sympathy and attention — as a fellow-soldier in the battle, or a fellow-traveller *in via*, I need quite a lot of my strength to survive myself; yet I must do *something*, or become less human.

So that intercessory prayer becomes, in the end, something like glancing at another sympathetically, touching another to bring comfort, holding another's hand, even hugging another — all things we do in common life at one time or another, according to the degree of distress we encounter.

This is, I suspect, a fairly low-grade form of intercessory prayer — yet I find myself wondering more and more if intercessory prayer is not designed to benefit those who do it rather than those to whom it is, so to speak, 'done', and, subjectively speaking, I must say it has an effect.

10: Grumbling at God

CANON FFRENCH-BEYTAGH delighted me by saying once that people often seemed to talk about prayer as if they were trying to 'stroke' God and put him in a good mood, whereas the Canon often used prayer as an opportunity to grumble at God. He is quite right, of course, though I never saw it before. I remember many a clergyman telling me about the 'prayer of thanksgiving'; but I can't think of one who urged the opposite, the 'prayer of complaint'.

Yet it has good precedents. The psalms, for instance, show a healthy tendency to grouse; and it was touching, all these centuries afterwards, to find the same Jewish sense of wholeness emerging in the musical *Fiddler on the Roof*, where the hero tells God in no uncertain terms how he feels about poverty, persecution and difficult relatives. Even St. Paul, who usually seems more British than Jewish, with his stiff upper lip and his hang-ups about women, remembers to count his shipwrecks and scourgings — doubtless so that he can remind God on a suitable occasion. And, of course, St. Teresa, on a famous occasion, let rip with a fine feminine scorn.

It is, I suppose, part of the 'child-likeness' that is so often urged upon Christians; for, if there is one thing all parents know about children, it is that they grumble a great deal, protesting, like the young Radletts in *The Pursuit of Love*, 'It's not fair'. As indeed it isn't. Most human lives contain a gruelling number of knocks, hurts and disappointments; and the real question is whether we swallow them down, pretending to ourselves and others that they haven't really happened, or admit them as the wounds they are.

This is no trivial point. One of the most telling points made against Christianity by psychoanalysts and others is that it too often encourages us to identify with the 'good' side of ourselves and pretend that the rest is not there at all. Most of us, in our daily struggles with the world, work up a lot of aggression; and if this never appears in our prayers (there is remarkably little space for it in the liturgy, if you think about it), then we are using prayer to fragment ourselves rather than make ourselves whole.

However childlike we are (and we are often unnervingly childlike), we are not 'good' children; and the point about a relationship with God is that we have space in it to discover that this is so, and not be overcome by the discovery. God, I suspect, is not mocked if we are silly enough to try to stroke him instead.

11: Prayer of Asceticism

ONE OF THE most interesting things to argue about for those who care about prayer and spirituality is what role asceticism has nowadays in the life of the Christian.

We have tended to note and deplore the masochism of the Alexandrian Fathers or medieval monasticism, and to fall over backwards to avoid any kind of Puritan excess. Yet I wonder if the deep masochistic strain in the human personality is so easily disposed of. Many who would never dream of serious fasting, for example, behave in ways which could be construed as unconscious self-punishment (becoming alcoholics, attempting suicide, failing professionally, becoming invalids, even contracting disastrous marriages); at least the suffering of the Desert Fathers was consciously self-inflicted, and therefore perhaps, had more potential for wholeness.

What is moving, over and over again, is the moment where the ascetic decides to give up his excess of self-mortification (discovering, like Hermann Hesse's 'Sidhartha', that it is a sort of drug). Led very often by the guidance of a feminine figure such as Sophia — or, as in the case of St. Seraphim of Sarov, the Virgin Mary — the hermit is taken from his torment of suffering on to a different level of living. It is as if the positive feminine principle has taken over from the negative one of masochism.

But the soul has learned the most important lesson of its life — the lesson of its poverty — and it is only out of the thoroughness of this agonising lesson that any real love for God or man can grow. It does not, at the moment, come very naturally to us to become hermits (though there is a growing movement in the Church concerned to re-discover the role of the hermit), yet out of our particular forms of suffering we can discern something new about our identity.

The asceticism of the Desert Fathers led them to an extraordinary simplicity and lack of pomposity, more particularly about prayer. 'A monk asked St. Macarius how to pray. The latter replied: "It is not necessary to use many words. Only stretch out your arms and say: Lord, have pity on me as you desire and as you well know how! And if the enemy presses you hard, say: Lord, come to my aid!" ' It is the utterance of a man who has reached and passed the boundaries of his own strength.

I am not suggesting that in order to pray we should take to hair shirts and chains; that is not our route. Only that when we get to that level of prayer, and of life, we shall know that we have found *our* route.

12: Prayer in the Group

ONE OF THE most interesting developments of our own time is our growing sense of the importance of the 'group'.

Nowadays it is quite difficult to escape being a member of a group of some kind, whether it is formed to protect its members against the world, to achieve some reforming objective, to further a political, cultural or spiritual cause, or simply to give its members a chance to know other people better. Given the large and impersonal societies in which many have to live, it is a way of rediscovering ourselves in relation to other people.

In the matter of prayer there are two ways in which the group can be important. One is the small group where the members meet together to pray, perhaps to share other concerns, perhaps just to learn something about the experience of collective silence, about which we are rather ignorant. The lonelinesses and fears of prayer might perhaps be met better by experiments of this kind than we are always ready to admit.

The continuing existence of the Church also takes for granted a much bigger group of which we cannot know all the members; and, precious as the personal is in all our lives, the impersonality of our membership of the body of the Church also has a value.

I welcome the impersonality of liturgical worship, and even the impersonality of many a church where one can drift in and out of a service almost invisibly, sensing in this not 'unfriendliness' (and, being shy myself, I never expect others to be any friendlier than I am) but a welcome tendency to 'let be'. In the river of the liturgy it seems possible to bathe one's weary little ego, and even for a moment to forget its existence and become part of the river instead.

I often find myself wishing that, alongside liturgical and sacramental insights, we could set some of the Quaker knowledge and experience of silence. Within the Church of England silence often seems to mean five minutes; and even that is nervously and arbitrarily interrupted with 'guiding' comments of one kind and another, as if the mind left idle is bound to get up to no good. While the transcendental meditators feel the need for two twenty-minute periods of silence a day, most of the Christians chatter on.

Do we want so much talk in our churches? And, even if the answer is yes, the simple faithful (those poor old scapegoats of all our failures) demand it, then what is to stop the complicated faithful from trying to learn collectively more about silence? I have a hunch that this is something we need to cultivate if we are to begin to take the measure of our present spiritual need.

13: The Conundrum of Prayer

I FEEL CONSIDERABLE sympathy for the clergy in the present post-Christian era, but never more so than when I hear them asked one of those unanswerable conundrums in which religion abounds. Conundrums are, and are meant to be, unanswerable; and perhaps the genuine response would be one of those unnerving rejoinders in which the Zen masters excelled — a swift slap, or a pail of water emptied over the pupil's head.

A favourite gambit in pupil-ship at the moment is to ask how to pray — the pupil wide-eyed and avid for a technique which, despite all his best endeavours, has hitherto evaded him. So popular is the question that transcendental meditation, which supplies an answer in the form of a technique, is a *succès fou.*

This is obviously useful. Anyone who is seriously interested in prayer must sooner or later struggle with set times and periods of withdrawl, and learn something of the physical and mental concomitants of prayer; and transcendental meditation, while being modest in its claims about what it does and does not do for the meditator, provides a serious answer for people who want to know 'what to do'.

What, however, makes the question 'How do I pray?' such an impossible conundrum is that, beneath the surface techniques, is the infinitely difficult question 'How can I be?' It is, of course, precisely this question that we are asking those to whom we turn for spiritual advice; and I think we are most fortunate if they, like the Zen masters, find a way to deflect the question and force it back upon ourselves.

Perhaps more than anything else we do, with the possible exception of the way we spend money, the way we pray indicates our state of being. Our fears, our rigidity, our inability to 'let go', our guilt, our loneliness, our anxiety, all rear their heads in prayer; and it is not altogether surprising that some Christians get phobic about it.

A good spiritual director, it seems to me, must be one who, like the good Freudian analyst, holds a mirror up to those who seek his advice. It is often embarrassing to have to reflect for another the side of themselves they are unconsciously showing; yet this is really what 'advice' consists of, since all else a man is capable of seeing for himself.

It is the seeing of this darker side of ourselves, like the dark side of the moon, that promotes 'enlightenment' or spiritual growth and makes it possible to move towards deeper prayer. There is an element of shock in it, as with the Zen master's cold water; but, if it teaches us that there is no real answer to the conundrum 'How do I pray?' except to get on with the painful (and laughable) task of being, we shall annoy one another less.

V

THE FOUR LAST THINGS

1: Death

EVERY GENERATION HAS its blind spot. Ours, it is now almost a platitude to suggest, is death.

Shielded as we are, in the West, from terrible realities of hunger and disease, we can censor death from our thoughts and our imaginations. 'Don't mention death,' a Fleet Street editor I once worked for used to say. It loses readers.' We seem to be trying to kid ourselves that we are going to live for ever.

Death becomes improper. We fight shy of the bereaved, and, where our ancestors would have wept with them, we become terrified of saying the wrong thing. We have no lore about preparing the dying, and often think that all we can do for them is to lie to them about their state of health. We are baffled by the plight of poorer nations where death by hunger is an ordinary occurrence.

I cannot speak for others, but I find myself ready to admit to real poverty when it comes to an understanding of death, an entire lack of education. Three years ago I found myself, for the first time in my life, confronted by the dead body of someone dear to me. The poorest citizens of the world could have responded as I could not. I feared to touch because of the stiffness I imagined common to all dead bodies. I was afraid to kiss the cheek in case it felt cold. Above all, I felt puzzled, ignorant, before the astonishing change that death had produced. It was the person I had known, and yet it wasn't.

I hated my awkwardness and fear, and yet that quiet body has stayed reassuringly in my memory since. So *that* was death, was it? — finally something so simple and so ordinary.

Not everyone, luckily, has been as sheltered as I have, yet I begin to sense a movement among Christians and others to go back to the school of death, there to become a willing, not a resentful, pupil. The thought occurs to me that, far from becoming morbid and gloomy, my life might be considerably enriched if I could learn 'the art of dying'.

It is, after all, part of the exceedingly difficult task that awaits the religious man — that of learning to trust. It is the final and the most important lesson. It is part of another and equally difficult undertaking — that of losing the self, our spurious, self-willed identity, in order to find it. Thomas Merton quoted a Buddhist poem: 'The King of Death does not see you if you do not see any self in yourself.'

What we fear in death is losing our shaky identity. If we have already willingly cast it aside (or anyhow made attempts to do so — few get further), then much of the terror of death is gone. Similarly, if we have learned to find meaning in our world, to discover from hour to hour and day to day that although we may suffer we are not abandoned, then it is possible to bear not just our deaths but the knowledge of the pain of others.

It is the kind of world in which the worst happens, and yet hope and love still reign victorious. Knowing that it is *that* kind of world not only makes death possible. It makes life possible.

2: Judgment

THE JUDGMENT OF God, with all its fearsome division between the saved and the damned, fascinated Christians for centuries. It does not fascinate us — the only sermons I have ever heard on hell-fire have all been in plays; and heaven is scarcely more popular as a subject for preachers. The thought of the Day of Judgment itself does not fill many of us with anxious terror, and we spend little thought on the stern and wrathful aspects of God.

This is a very profound change of consciousness, and I wonder if it is only by chance that it coincides with a change in the behaviour of fathers. Fathers are no longer the all-powerful figures they once were, wielding corporal punishment and absolute authority. In such circumstances a father's disapproval was a death-dealing matter, as Luther so well illustrates; and bitterness, fear, rage, though also a longing for acceptance, crept easily into a man's feelings about God. Our view of God, by contrast, tends to be of an amiable, understanding figure — amiable as most fathers nowadays would prefer to be.

But, apart from the change in the role of fathers, there is, I think, another reason for our neglect of judgment. Our understanding of human wrong doing has also undergone a change. We may still be very muddled by what we actually believe — how far we think a man is master of his fate, and how far he is shaped by circumstances; but everyone seems agreed that human behaviour is more complex than it once seemed to be. It would not occur to us, as it did to our ancestors, to expose the drunkard, the scold, the thief, the adulterer, to public ridicule or worse. We may not like what they do, but we sense that the springs of such conduct are mysterious and imperfectly understood by us.

And so we tend to have no language in which to speak of judgment, and thus ignore it, I think, to our great impoverishment. The rejecting, hypercritical and disparaging father has been thrown overboard on the human voyage, and a good job too, but guilt remains; and, because it is vague, unpersonalised, undirected guilt, it settles into a miserable, chronic complaint. We have no hope of the catharsis of an Augustine, a Luther or a Bunyan.

One thing seems certain — we cannot go backwards, as those

who rail at 'the permissive society' seem often to forget. But how to go forwards?

First, by looking at the moral giants of our society and seeing what drives them. The moral giants of our time seem to be those who act not from fear or guilt, or out of obedience to any collective norm, but out of obedience to their personal vocation. 'Integrity' is our word for faithful obedience to this vocation, the vocation of the man who picks his way through the temptations of the modern world — supremely the temptations of money, power, fame and greed.

Solzhenitsyn carried his own judgment within him — he had no choice, since he lived in a corrupt society. He refused (among so many other brave choices) to commit suicide, not because any collective told him it was wrong, but because he had personally hammered out that conclusion. He needed no threatening father to make him good; the day of judgment worked in his own soul.

Most of us are not in that class. Will we behave well if Dad is not there to beat us? It is, in a sense, too late to ask that question any more. *All* society is breaking down around us; and, if it has not yet gone as far here as it has in Russia, few observers can be very sanguine about what is to come.

In this situation all collectives, even the collectives which most loudly proclaim moral rectitude, are our particular devil, Nuremberg rallies of the spirit, luring us away from the pain of integrity into the cosy womb of hysteria. The real test of whether we have taken judgment into our very being is what we can do alone, with no collective to soothe us. Unless we can find the courage to undertake our journeys into integrity, then we are judged and found wanting; socially, if not individually, we are damned men.

3: Hell

HELL HAS A strange way of redefining itself from generation to generation. Trying to find a synonym for hell, I thought instantly of 'bondage'.

Not torture, though fantasies of torture have played a big part in Christian thinking about hell. Torture is only a part. Deliberate physical injury, terrible as it is, is only incidental to the major misery: that of not being free to get up and walk away or to choose some alternative course of action.

And whereas physical torture, even in our own dark times, happens only to a minority, those who know at first hand about bondage are very many. We are bound in so many ways — through our relationships, our prejudices, our temperaments, our fears, through our need to earn money or to win social acceptance. I cannot think of anyone who seems to me a free man, though I can think of many who have 'patches' of freedom in whose ambience the rest of us can snatch a little temporary freedom. But we all know, inside ourselves, about hell, and how its bondage makes us suffer.

What is surprising about our ancestors' view of hell is that they were so sure it was a divinely inflicted form of suffering, whereas, if there is one insight that recurs in the twentieth century with unceasing monotony, it is that we choose bondage. It becomes harder and harder to pretend that bondage happens to us against our will and inclination; the fact is that we are terrified of freedom, whereas bondage (hell) is totally secure though extremely unpleasant.

Yet the way to freedom is such a strange 'Through the

Looking-Glass' affair that we can have no more than odd flashes of intuition about how to get there. Beating on the walls and wanting to get out doesn't help a bit, though we all do it. Trying to be good is useless, though some of us do that too. Resignation is inhuman, perhaps a sort of suicide.

The way out of bondage is so drastic that you can see why people lose their nerve. The way to get out is to give up autonomy, to become totally, trustingly, content to let one's tiny identity become a satellite around the bigger 'I' which gives it the only identity it has. (This may only be possible when exhaustion from trying to 'go it alone' has set in.) It means surrendering the endless wanting which makes up most of our lives, since without wanting there is, amazingly, no bondage.

Freedom is unnervingly close, a freedom which no human prison and no human authority can take away, a freedom before which death itself must give way. It is this which all the great religions of the world have tried to articulate, helping to release men from their superstitious attempts to 'magic' and manipulate the world to their own advantage. *That* is slavery. We must move beyond that kind of compulsion.

'Since, in truth, bondage and freedom are relative,' says an Indian writer, 'these words are only for those terrified with the universe. This universe is a reflection of minds. As you see many suns in water from one sun, so see bondage and liberation.'

Bondage is a reflection of something in our own minds, as the pictures of the tortures of the damned were a reflection of something in the minds of medieval artists. If we know that, we can begin to move out of the lurid lights of hell and into the cool dawn of the Resurrection.

4: Heaven

HELL IS, IN a sense, incurable hunger, and heaven is the absence of that hunger. I say absence rather than fullness because fullness suggests a full-stomached, cat-in-front-of-the-fire sort of contentment, and I don't think heaven is that, though I am not at all averse to it.

But the best thing about fullness, of any kind, is not the fullness itself but the freedom that flows from it. The hungry man can think of nothing but food. Feed him, and he does not go on thinking about food; his mind is freed to range over all kinds of other thoughts.

In our everyday human state we spend much of our lives suffering from one hunger or another, and perhaps are only released from this when love, in one of its many forms, lifts us out of our anxious preoccupations and on to a new level of experience altogether. Suddenly we are secure, not because someone has guaranteed us £5,000 a year for life or because we know we'll get a pension, but because another person shows that they love us, or because we get a sudden insight that love is the mysterious process that sustains us every moment of time.

And mysterious it is. Why should love, which can often do us no practical good, make a difference to creatures like ourselves whose specific needs apparently are for food and warmth and oxygen? I can't pretend I know; but, just as Mark Twain could live for a month on a good compliment, so the friendliness, the sympathy, the concern, the interest, of others can carry us through private famines which would otherwise kill us. Is that heaven then? Well, not quite, but it can open for us a door into a new territory which I believe is heaven. We cannot bear to open the door very fast or very far at first — freedom and joy are more alarming to old lags like us than we imagine from inside our prisons — but we can learn with the help of those who love us to allow a little more of the radiance to touch us.

What I am trying to say is that heaven is not a passive state, a return to the womb in which we are fed without effort, but is rather a movement into total response. The spiritual life is a slow, and often agonising, process of 'coming alive' in which one part of us after another emerges from inertia into trembling and passionate life. Much of the time we would rather it wasn't happening — we were happy enough with our old partial identity and our vegetable existence. We know that to become more conscious means to suffer more, and we forget that it also makes us more capable of experiencing joy.

In the end it comes down to obedience — not to some arbitrary authority, but to the journey that summons each one of us. Heaven, as the old rhyme used to say, is our destination, that state of discovered and fulfilled identity which is inseparable from our discovery of God and *his* identity. We stumble upon little bits of it all the time, but in our blasé, over-sophisticated way we make light of this everyday miracle, blinded by our fear and our activity and our greed.

We are not very good at cultivating awareness except under the stress of great emotion, but we can never quite forget about heaven while we have to live with our poverty, our hunger, our little hells of emptiness and inadequacy which continually remind us of their opposite. And, while in our poverty, we are comforted by the love of others. In this we are luckier than the rich men who lose the kingdom of heaven from absent-mindedness.

VI

SEVEN UNCERTAINTIES

1: "Christian Answers" Tend to Oversimplify

TRYING TO TELL the Editor what I had in mind for this series, I used the shorthand, 'hot potatoes': that is to say, the sort of subjects that *Church Times* readers get most worked up about in the correspondence columns. Abortion and women priests were the first two that came to mind, with divorce, homosexuality and extramarital sex following hard on their heels.

I think that what drove me on to write the series, as well as to give it its rather tentative title, was the feeling that I have not got these questions worked out to anything like my own satisfaction, and that I need to think about them a lot more.

Of course I know that even to wonder and puzzle about them causes offence in certain quarters — the quarters where there is a 'Christian answer' to every question. But what worries me about 'Christian answers' of that kind is that they nearly always seem to be 'tough' (not to say brutal) answers, giving blanket commands to people to do what often turns out to be the impossible; and my experience of life does not lead me to think that this is the way of love.

Blanket answers seem, superficially, to be based on appeals either to the Bible or to 'authority'; but underneath I sometimes think I discern an overwhelming attraction to 'simplicity' of thought. It really is so much simpler, neater, if you condemn, for example, all abortion whatever the reason, and give it a title like 'murder'. You then do not have to bear the agonising uncertainties and doubts, possibly the guilts. It asks of you no inner struggle, no admission of conflicting or upsetting evidence; you simply do either what your own emotions, or some external 'authority', tells you is the 'right' thing to do.

I am no moral theologian, but I have slowly and painfully come to the conviction that there are no simplicities, and no blanket answers; and, if we want to love others and not rush them into quick, and bad, solutions, then we have to remain open to all kinds of answers — some of them personally upsetting and offensive, no doubt.

What is so hard for every one of us to believe is that others are not made like us (quite apart from the fact that they exist in entirely different situations), and that life is not neat but messy, as well as being paradoxical, contradictory and full of surprise. This is why we need an extraordinary mental flexibility in looking at everything from moral questions to the economic situation, trying to perceive in the tangle of threads the one that will lead us home.

I don't pretend to have sharper eyes than the next man, or to be exempt from the most ludicrous prejudices which make me blush with shame when someone catches me out in them. And I really do not know the 'answer' in any of the questions I want to discuss, since I find the radical 'let's be daring and say the opposite of what the others say' just as unhelpful and basically heartless as the conservative 'let's go on saying what we always said'.

Neither really wants the suffering of the human situation, and so they dodge by taking an extreme position. What they also dodge, it seems to me, is a living experience of faith, an ability to go on in a state of blindness, doubt and genuine 'not knowing'. If we will not let go of certainty, then there is a sense in which we can never grow up.

Let me come clean about my attitudes to the subjects mentioned above, so that you can see where my bias lies.

I do not feel able to utter a blanket condemnation of all abortions, all divorce, all homosexuality or all extramarital sex, though I can think of many situations where I would deplore one or more of them in practice. Because orthodox opinion has been so strongly against them, and because I have an immense respect both for Biblical insights and for Church teaching, I feel obliged to question myself continually and not to adopt any sort of complacent attitude. But, the more I question and the more I look at actual situations, the more I continue to feel that sometimes the 'hard' and sometimes the 'soft' solution is the right one.

Women priests are obviously a different matter. Individuals, *pace* those eleven brave women and their bishops in America, cannot opt out of the collective view in this matter, more especially since they seek to minister within that collective. But here surely we need to think much more deeply about male/female roles, as well as about the extraordinary priestly function many women have long performed (unpaid) in the Church, and as well as wondering much harder what the priest's function really is.

Since I have already stuck my neck out, let me stick it out a few inches farther and say that I do not believe there is a 'Christian answer' to anything at all; and I deplore the tendency to 'make man for the Sabbath' that suggests that there is. All that is available to us is a 'human answer', one that exists in the same way for those who are not practising Christians as for those who are; and it is an answer (if I have understood Christ at all) which tries to set pre-judgments on one side and see what is the most loving solution for the greatest number of people.

Sometimes a loving solution can cause agonising and guilt-producing feelings (as in the decision to end a marriage which is no more than a sham) yet which are unavoidable. Sometimes it can produce the sort of self-sacrifice with which Christians have tended to feel more at home. I don't believe that there's a hard-and-fast rule, only the rule of people's human and spiritual growth. And a painful business *that* is.

2: The Problem of Abortion

ABORTION IS A subject which sets the nerves twanging of many besides Christians. Not surprisingly, when you think of it, since the urge to conceive, carry, give birth to and cherish human life is one of the deepest of human instincts. We cannot treat the embryo as cheap and worthless without passing judgment on all human life, including our own. Sexual intercourse, pregnancy, childbirth are the most moving (and, I would add, sacramental) experiences some of us have had; and we cannot think of a baby, or even an embryo, without reverence and awe.

But it seems to me that it is *because* a baby is potentially so important, because it matters, that the worrying and guilt-producing decision to have an abortion may sometimes be the right one, though it is one that most of us would rather be spared. Indeed, if we live in reasonably comfortable conditions, have a partner who loves us, access to efficient contraceptives (together with enough intelligence and emotional balance to be able to use them), we probably are spared.

Many people, however, who have recourse to abortion are not so fortunate. They may be homeless, or live in appalling conditions. They may have husbands who have already proved themselves to be disastrous fathers and providers, or have discovered that they themselves cannot cope with the children they already have. They may drink or take drugs, or suffer from mental or physical illnesses which preclude motherhood. They may know very well that they should not conceive in such conditions; but, as has been shown over and over again, the worse people's living conditions, the more readily they conceive.

A common 'Christian' answer to these arguments (and I find it hard to see it as other than a cynical one) is that living conditions must be improved. But most Christians lack the resources to rehouse large numbers of people or heal the wounds of personality which afflict them, and in the meantime pious resolves do nothing to help *this* particular woman who has the problem now.

To make it all more complicated there is another group who have frequent recourse to abortion not because of social deprivation or inadequacy, nor from lack of intelligence, but from an extraordinary carelessness (or do I mean callousness?) in the whole matter of intercourse and contraception.

I can think of one young woman, not in the least deprived socially, who has had three abortions in three years — lacking, it seems, in any sense of the wonder and beauty of human life, and certainly lacking in guilt. I cannot wonder at hospital staffs feeling a sense of rage and exploitation when they see patients such as her return time after time, monopolising our scarce and precious medical resources and treating an unborn baby as little more than an appendix.

Finally, there is the older woman whose children may be nearly grown up and who may feel her years of bearing and caring for children are long past. Suddenly confronted with an unlooked-for pregnancy, she feels that she *cannot* go through with it. In some cases she does go through with it, and all is well. As the anti-abortion lobby say: 'You love it when it comes.'

But it is not always so simple. I have in my possession a letter from a woman of sixty who bitterly resents the presence of a twelve-year-old son in her household, and cannot resist showing him her resentment. A friend of mine, deeply troubled all her life with mysterious neurotic symptoms, only discovered in adult life that her mother had never wanted her and had deeply resented her birth. Her mother never admitted this to her, and forced herself to pretend a love she did not feel; but the child was not wholly deceived.

I have described three very different groups who turn to abortion — the socially deprived, the cynically callous and the older woman — but what they all have in common is one thing: they do not wish to bear a child. I feel that we are fooling ourselves if we pretend that, when the little bundle arrives, all will automatically become well. *Sometimes* all becomes well. Sometimes the outcome is a Maria Colwell, or a child damaged to a greater or lesser degree by unloving parental attitudes.

What I believe Christians have to ask themselves is: do we believe that life, *any* life, is worth preserving at any cost? (We do not appear to think so in other contexts; for example, by no means all Christians are pacifists.) Was it really better for Maria Colwell to be born than not to be born, and is it better for the many who can only come into a little hell upon earth? Would any of us choose to be born to a mother who was casually promiscuous, not mature enough even to bother *not* to have a child she doesn't want? Would we wish to be born to a mother who was mentally disturbed, or too ill to care for us properly? Would we wish to grow up 'in care', or in and out of any number of foster-homes?

If you love life it is terribly painful to have to make decisions which end it, whether it is speeding an old lady through an agonising terminal illness with larger-than-normal helpings of drugs, or helping a menopausal woman terminate a pregnancy she emphatically does not want (and many GPs and others have to make such decisions on our behalf). Yet surely the point of the Christian gospel is that the story does not end with each individual life, whether tragic or fulfilled — that there is more to our existence than the few years of our life upon earth.

Death, whether for an embryo or an old man, is not the whole story, and Christians, of all people, cannot believe that life on any terms is necessarily the best of all alternatives. What Christians strive for is life informed by love; and love, it seems to me, often denies us the 'pure decisions' which we would prefer, and enjoins us to shades of grey, to doubts, uncertainties and twinges of guilt. If we are loving we cannot be 'all good'; we can only do the best we can and help others (often driven by pressures beyond our imagining) to do the best *they* can.

3: The Church's Attitude to Women

A FEW WEEKS ago, on holiday in Wales, I visited Caldey Island with my family. As we got off the boat our eyes were met by a large notice which read: 'Tours of the monastery are at the following times ... Women are not permitted to enter.'

'What are they afraid we'll do?' my teenage daughter and her friend asked with interest. I found it hard to answer, for behind such a notice is a way of thinking about women that stretches back to medieval times and beyond. According to this way of thinking woman is the temptress, the archetypal Eve. Let her in, and she will wreak havoc — the havoc of painful fantasy in men's minds, if not of any other kind. Yet this view tends to exist side by side with a very different view of woman, idealised almost out of flesh-and-blood existence. I found myself recalling that the Cistercians have a 'special devotion' to the Virgin Mary.

These two alternative views of women have, I suggest, played an inordinate part in Christian thinking and continue to play a residual part to this day, even though few Christian institutions nowadays would admit their prejudices quite as openly as Caldey. What always seems to have been difficult for Christianity (and for some other religions, it must be admitted) is to see women as *people*, not simply as screens upon which male fantasies or ideals could be projected. St. Paul's famous comment that it was better to marry than to burn (though no doubt showing a compassionate understanding of his male disciples) is terrifying in its callousness about women. Women existed solely to save men from the bothersome distraction of desire.

We have learned a great deal about sexuality since St. Paul's day — not least that, whether we like it or not, it occupies a central position in the lives of men and women. We can recognise it or we can repress it (with consequent neurotic complications), but we can no longer treat it as unimportant or a distraction from the business of the Kingdom. It belongs, as all things human belong, in the Kingdom.

But, because of past misunderstandings and *gaucherie* in the matter of women and sexuality, the Church, I suggest, now has a formidable task ahead of it. It is the task of rethinking its attitudes to women, and to their religious function in particular. (There is also the matter of rethinking its attitude to sexuality, but I will come to that in later articles.) And, when I say the Church, I mean (I wish I didn't) you and me.

Two kinds of women have, as I have said, recurred with eerie frequency in the Christian imagination — fallen women (those upon whom we have projected desires we didn't want to recognise) and virgins (our idealised selves). It is time now, I think, for our imaginations to leave these extremes (with the splitting of the personality they express) and to recognise that the love which the majority of women give, and which, I believe, is one of the truly creative forces of our society, is of a very different order indeed.

In true sexual relationships, women are infinitely more than an alternative to 'burning'. Innumerable husbands could testify to the creative power of their wife's love, as others, whose wives despise or fear sex, could testify to this potential healing by its absence. Yet this is not, or not yet, a natural and accepted part of Christian thinking.

'I know you won't agree,' a visiting workman said to the wife of a clergyman friend of mine, 'but I think my wife's hands are the hands of God.' The Christians are not expected to understand about the word made flesh.

Nor, of course, is a fulfilling sexual relationship woman's only spiritual function. Other civilizations and religions than our own have repeatedly recognised that women have special insights, a shaman-like vision; that, given the chance, they perform a healing and priestly function all their own. Arrogantly we Christians talk disparagingly of pagan 'priestesses'; are we so sure that the pagan cultures did not have something we have lost, an awareness that there are 'mysteries' vital to our spiritual health which are the province of woman, just as there are 'mysteries' which are the province of men?

What I believe the almost total masculinisation of our churches has led to (in terms of leadership and priestly function) is a huge and tragic impoverishment of Christianity. Men need the 'feminine principle' (what Jung called the 'anima') to enable them to create and to grow; and, if they are led to exclude it, or despise it, or deny it, then lack of imagination, dullness and finally deadness overtake them.

This is not, as you might think, a plea for the instant ordination of women; indeed I rather fear that, if that happened, women might become a carbon copy of the priesthood we already have, and I would like to see something different evolve. I believe the first step towards it would be for women to be *valued* more in the churches and given more chance to exercise their ministries.

Many women, for example, have real gifts as listeners and counsellors ('confessors' is the word Christians have used), gifts which are often of particular importance for men; yet this has little official recognition. Again others have begun to show great distinction in the field of theology, yet few paths seem open to them to allow them to share this knowledge with their fellow-Christians.

Few cathedrals seem to think of offering women canonries (perhaps their statutes make this difficult; I don't know) or their equivalent; yet, if we want to progress beyond the *apartheid* of Caldey, then women must be valued not just in words but in terms of money and jobs and opportunities. The Church must, as it were, put its money where its mouth is. I believe the result would enrich us all, both men and women.

4: Sex Before Marriage

I THINK IT was John Wilson who pointed out that the English language has no word which comes, as it were, between promiscuous and chaste. If you are not promiscuous then you are chaste, and if you are not chaste you are promiscuous — an odd quirk of language which owes more to the rather wistful Christian sexual ideal than to the reality of life as most of us observe it around us.

For, even if we take the line that many Christians do that marriage is a form of chastity (a little oddly, I always think — my dictionary defines chaste as 'virgin' and 'abstaining from intercourse'), it can scarcely be accurate to describe as promiscuous, i.e. indiscriminate, someone who has three or four deeply-loved partners in the course of a lifetime, whether married to them or not.

This gap in our language, and therefore in our thinking, is being brought home to us in an acute form by our young people, and more particularly by the student generation — that is, those who have to wait longest for marriage. When I was that age only the most daring young people, at least in my circle, slept openly together; a girl was told that she must 'keep herself for marriage' and that her husband 'wouldn't respect her' if she was no longer a virgin — a fairly powerful disincentive.

It was partly to do with religion (I remember a clergyman telling me when I was about twenty that the choice before me was either marriage or life-long chastity, which made me feel I must get a husband at all costs), but also to do with social convention. Thus my parents, who had no particular religion, would have been just as horrified as the clergyman if I had broken the convention.

The world has changed a great deal in the intervening twenty years, and in nothing has it changed faster than in the refusal of young people to accept the taboo on premarital sex. I have a number of young student friends; and, as soon as they know me well enough, they begin to tell me of the boy or girl they live with and boys and girls their friends live with. You couldn't call it promiscuity and you couldn't call it chastity — more a recognition that it is pleasant and natural to make love within an ongoing relationship, but that poverty and extreme youth are not a basis for a life-long union.

It is not easy for traditional Christians to know what to make of these semi-permanent liaisons, so firmly have we believed that the only positive alternatives open to a Christian believer were those which I was offered in youth. Yet I see in many of these young people a real devotion to their partner, and a real healing of the wounds and self-doubts of adolescence that probably could take place in no other way. I also see that these partners are not necessarily the ones who will be right for them at twenty-five, still less at forty-five.

Such liaisons carry a lot of joy and pain, and joy and pain lead to growth. Looking at them, I cannot feel that my own inhibited youth, with the ever-present need to 'take care', was a better introduction to life and love than theirs. Yes, I do know that some of these liaisons lead to tragedy of one kind and another, but there were tragedies in my youth too — tragedies of extreme inhibition, of couples who married 'just for sex', and of 'shotgun' marriages.

But what, in the face of these empirical observations, can I say of the long and rigid Christian tradition of absolute premarital chastity? First, that it expressed a real and precious insight that sexual desire can be destructive, that *real* promiscuity encourages a split between love and desire that erodes relationship.

Second, that it expressed an ambivalence about women. On the one hand it protected them from the ravages of male desire at a time when no reliable contraceptives were available to them. On the other hand it viewed them not so much as persons as property to be handed over intact from father to husband (the sub-plot of *Much Ado about Nothing* reveals this in a peculiarly chilling form), with relationship seen only as a lucky incidental.

Third — and from our point of view much the most important, since this is where we have to start thinking and questioning — it ignored the positive value of sexuality, grudgingly allowing it as a practical necessity within marriage for the 'procreation' of children but implying that in an ideal world everyone would live like a monk.

It is this latter Muggeridgean view that some of us feel a need to reject both in our own lives and, so far as we can influence them, in the lives of others. That sex can be healing and joyful (sometimes outside marriage as well as in it), that it can lead to personal growth, that it is a way of knowing God, above all that it is *good*, still takes a certain nerve to say in Christian circles; and I have no doubt that I shall undergo the usual penalties for saying it.

But the repressive and sex-hating voices still seem to dominate our discussion of sexual morals, and it seems important that other voices should speak up. For it is, I have come to believe, by knowing the wonderful goodness of sexuality and by valuing it as we value all good things, that we can work best against those who try to make it trivial or impersonal. If we despise the body and its delights, we open the way to the cynical exploiters.

5: Marriage — and Putting Asunder

AS A CHILD I used to feel envy when I saw a bride coming out of church. I wanted a long white dress with a veil like that, and, even more, I wanted the romantic love which I imagined invariably accompanied the union.

Such a childish view obviously had to go, but what it has given way to over the years is not so much disappointment or disillusionment at the loss of an ideal — as I shall say in a later article, I believe ideals are the Christian idols — as amazement at the casualness, even carelessness, of our marriage system. Marriage is still, in our society, the basis of the family (and personally I hope it may long continue to be so), and we still regard the family as our most important unit.

We have an ever-increasing flow of evidence that upon the wellbeing of this unit depends the mental and physical health of the next generation. Upon the relationship between parents, and the relationship of parents to their children, hangs the child's ability to relate to other people, and, eventually, its ability to control its greed, its aggressiveness, its sexual desires and its criminal wishes.

Almost nothing, then, is as important as marriage; indirectly it affects crime, war, mental and physical sickness, inflation and, supremely, the loving capacity of the next generation. Yet (and I can scarcely believe it even as I write it down) we give it about as much critical attention and interest as, say, poultry-farming — also, I am told, in a parlous state at the moment.

Why? I have no doubt that there are deep, unconscious reasons, but, since I am as unconscious of them as everyone else, I can only offer superficial reasons.

One is that we are intensely sentimental about marriage. We like to think of people marrying 'for love' without unpacking that tricky word, which can mean almost anything. We like all the paraphernalia of church weddings (agnostics loved Princess Anne's wedding just as much as the rest of us did), and, through the mist of happy tears and the rain of confetti and the water-fall of champagne, it is not easy to see or think all that clearly. Only — maybe marriage is too important for sentimentality, and maybe we should remember old Jung's warning that sen-timentality and cruelty are invariably found together.

Second, there has been the feeling that marriage was the Church's business — it is one of the few areas where the Church's authority is still extensively acknowledged — so that whatever our society was doing had a kind of seal of approval on it. This might have been the cue for the Church to attempt the most radical reappraisal of our marriage system in the light of the vast change in the status of women and twentieth-cen-tury insights about sexuality and relationship, but in fact the whole hit-or-miss system has continued unchanged, like a cot-tage industry ignoring the Industrial Revolution, until finally starvation and suffering force us into a cry of despair.

One of the biggest brakes to a compassionate grappling with the problems of marriage is that, however the problem is stated, the Western Churches (not the Eastern, I believe) have decided we must come up with the answer in the back of the book. Divorce is out of the question. Or it is allowed in a grudging, oh-what-a-lousy-Christian-you-are spirit that is almost more offensive than an outright raspberry.

Reading the *Report of the Commission on the Christian Doctrine of Marriage (1971)* I had the impression that its authors, despite their best endeavours for magnanimity, felt they were sucking on a collective lemon. Those who divorce have offended against 'the sanctity of marriage'; they have let the side down. Christians are not supposed to make mistakes, and, if they do, then the 'better way' is to conceal their failure from the world.

Personally, I question this view of the Christian. I feel he is someone who should be *more* ready to admit to failure than the next man, that it is the recognition of his essential poverty which is his passport to the kingdom. Divorce should in a sense be easier for him than for the next man, because he does not feel obliged to keep up a front — a 'standard', as they call it — to the world.

He knows that man is a poor thing, and that he makes mistakes, but that in God's goodness they can still become part of a creative process. What he can't tolerate, or should not, is sham, loss of integrity, the pretence that all is well when it isn't. That kind of nonsense was the trap which held the poor old Pharisees.

So what about the 'indissolubility' of marriage? Should we not ask what in fact, makes for 'indissolubility'? Is it a matter of being married in church by a clergyman? Hardly, since in the early Church marriage was celebrated without benefit of clergy (according to Schillebeeckx). Is it a matter of vows? Not entirely, since, as Jack Dominian so cogently demonstrated in an appendix to the Commission's report, people are promising, in all good faith, what in many cases is not in their psychological power to give; and there can be no contract if one does not possess what one promises to give.

What makes marriage indissoluble, I hope we may one day come to see, is a quality of relationship. Innumerable couples achieve this despite (or rather because of) quarrels, difficulties, upheavals and pain. A minority do not achieve it, but can sometimes manage to achieve it with another partner if they are given the chance.

So there are two crucial questions which confront us. One is, what do we do about that minority? Do we encourage them to continue a non-relationship, a lie, a 'living in sin' in so far as the world believes they have a real relationship? Or do we give them every assistance with the agonising experience of separating, praising them for their integrity and recognising that this is *their* spiritual journey, a kind of 'going out' into the desert that has respectable Christian ancestry?

Second, what do we do about building up a much more realistic understanding of what the marital relationship needs for at least minimum success? (A surprising amount of work has been done on what makes a marriage almost certain to fail, but little or nothing is known of it by the general public.) A few lessons at school, a few preparation classes in the Vicar's study are derisory when you think that what is at stake is a lifetime of happiness or unhappiness.

What is needed is a whole-hearted joining of religious insights, counselling insights and psychoanalytic insights in an educational and counselling enterprise of so far unattempted proportions. The resentments and suspicions which all the relevant bodies have of one another are not an encouraging start; and, in addition to these, there is our deep-rooted fear of sex, fear of change, and, above all, fear of the devastating operation of love. But, if we are ever to free ourselves of the hypocritical cat's cradle in which we are entangled at the moment, we shall need courage and honesty. And, again, honesty.

6: Homosexuality

WHEN I SHOWED him an earlier article in this series which dealt principally with premarital sex, the editor of the *Church Times* commented that he felt my ideas on what Christians thought about sex were out of date. They *did* nowadays think that it was a good and creative thing, at least within marriage, and to suggest that to them it was a sort of regrettable necessity was to do them less than justice.

But it is precisely the insistence that only marital sex can possibly be good that gives rise to my suspicions, since this says that sex can only be good and creative if strictly confined within contractual obligations. Sex can, of course, be very good in such circumstances, but my observation of life does not lead me to believe that outside them it necessarily undergoes a dramatic change. What to me seems to control the goodness or otherwise is the relationship between the partners, so that sometimes sex does seem to be good outside marriage and sometimes to be bad within it.

The acid test of whether Christians *really* believe in the goodness of sex, however, lies in their attitude to homosexuality. Homosexuality has not got the practical grounds of pro-creation to recommend it to Christians (though, in an over-populated world, heterosexuals may turn out to be not so much 'practical' as more a dangerous nuisance). Unlike heterosex, the only thing to recommend it is that it brings joy and relief from loneliness to the many men and women who love their own sex. (Of course, like heterosex, it has many practitioners who are incapable of love or real personal response, but they are not the subject of this article). So that it poses the question to Christians in what I am afraid I must call a 'naked' form — do we or don't we believe that sexual practice informed by love is a good thing?

It is, of course, perfectly possible to dodge the whole issue by going off into what it says in Romans, or what happened to Sodom and Gomorrah, or what it is alleged happened to the Roman Empire. But I only attempt to write for people who do not assume that the Bible is invariably infallible, and who accept that human understanding of sexuality has undergone a revolution. We know things that St. Paul didn't, and in the light of our knowledge are bound to re-examine our beliefs.

What we know is that many decent, intelligent, moral and apparently normal people find their own sex more exciting than the opposite sex. Some are incapable of enjoying intercourse with the opposite sex; some can enjoy either. They are found in all walks of life, and in all professions — not a few of them among the priesthood of the Church of England.

If homosexuals, and bi-sexuals, belong to the Church, and want to live within its disciplines, what exactly do we expect them to do? Live a life of total celibacy, which most of us would prefer not to do? Or, like the rest of us, find what happiness they can?

People respond differently to the information, or the implication, that their sexual inclinations are 'wicked'. Some do pay the heavy price of total celibacy. Others, refusing to deny their deepest feelings whatever names others give to them, embark upon relationship with their own sex. But, because the atmosphere of 'sin' still clings around such practice, sadly many still feel a need to conceal their sexual orientation from their families, or from acquaintances they do not yet know well enough to trust. It is not surprising that groups like Gay Lib, resenting this heavy burden homosexuals have been asked to carry, become increasingly aggressive in their insistence that the rest of us overcome our prejudices.

But what seems strikingly obvious about all this is not how sad it is (most homosexuals are no sadder than anyone else), but how absurd it all is. How absurd it is that thousands of people are somehow 'not acceptable', sexually speaking, when all they want to do is something as relatively harmless as sex. This old taboo has reduced so many to depression, loneliness, shame, despair and suicide in the past that maybe the time has come at last to refuse its destructive dominance, and to admit that men's sexual tastes differ as widely as do their other tastes.

Since frankness seems more useful in this area than in most I should just like to add that, although my own sexual adjustment happens to be heterosexual, I can remember at least two occasions in my life when I have felt a passing physical attraction to a woman, and wished I had the courage at the very least to attempt an embrace. Was this rather nice feeling 'homosexuality', with all the extraordinary overtones the word has acquired over the centuries? I guess it must have been. And, if I had not been chicken and had embraced the women, would I have committed a sin, or made two rather lonely women happier?

Hard to say, but common sense suggests to me the latter. Unless, of course, they themselves were so bound by the taboo that they had merely slapped my face.

7: Pornography

I WAS IN MY late teens before I discovered pornography — they didn't have it in the local library, and at my girls' grammar school sex never seemed to rear its head in any form except in the Bible and in the classics. So that one day I paused to look in a book shop window in a turning off the Strand and was mightily surprised at the contents. I can only remember one title now — Flogging in the British Army Through the Ages, or words to that effect; but that and the other titles together added up to a shock which I still remember all these years later.

I was a naive child by present-day standards, with no knowledge of the strange by-ways into which sexual desire can lead people and only a vague theoretical knowledge of the straight high road, so that the set of wares in the window brought home to me with sudden clarity a small set of truths.

First, that sex was of much more interest and importance in people's lives than I had been brought up to believe. Second, that it was linked with other functions and emotions that I had never associated with sex at all. Third, and by far the most worrying, whereas some of the titles baffled me, and still do, others struck unexpected chords of knowledge and awareness. The flogging book, for instance, reminded me of a film I had seen — I think it was probably the old Charles Laughton movie, Hunchback of Notre Dame — with a flogging scene that I had actually found disturbingly exciting.

This is all very old-fashioned, because any child of the same age nowadays knows a great deal more about sex than I knew, including deviant sex, and has probably seen films infinitely more sadistic than Hunchback. I mention the incident, though, because I use it as a memento of something easy to forget, something I often do forget: that what shocks and disgusts me most deeply in pornography is that it reminds me of emotions I have already experienced and feel guilty about.

The flogging book shocked me, and remained in my memory, because I know about sadistic feeling; it told me an unpalatable truth about myself. Other books and themes that others would find disturbing, made no impact upon me and have faded from my memory.

It seems to be generally true about pornography that it excites the already corrupted (often, if we despise our corruption, to our extreme annoyance), but that it leaves the uncorrupted parts of us (and all of us have these too) untouched, puzzled, possibly mildly amused. This is not to welcome the stuff with open arms. I do not particularly want my children to look at pornography, probably because I fear the painful feeling it may evoke in them; and I don't look at it myself, except when it accidentally comes my way, because I know that it does not bring me joy. But I do not really understand the extraordinary anxiety Christians often bring to the subject, because I don't believe it is what corrupts people.

I rather wish it was what corrupted people, because then the remedy would be so delightfully simple; but the situation is, in reality, complex and tragic. It is that our corruption (that is our distortion of warm, generous sexuality) goes far deeper than photographs or films or salacious literature. Long before we get to the point of looking at such things – I would guess in the first few years of life and in our relation to our parents — patterns of sadism, of masochism, of fetishism and obsession are laid down, and it is these primitive patterns that the pornographers so profitably exploit.

So what are we to do as the floods of pornography rise ever higher about us? I hesitate to say this in the *Church Times,* where I have read a number of portentous statements on the subject, but my first thought is: laugh about it. I don't mean laugh in a superior way (and none of that hypocrisy about pornography being 'boring' either; it can be compulsively interesting), but laugh at ourselves and the poor, mixed-up creatures we turn out to be, just as Christianity always said we were.

Second, ask *why* so many men and women, and boys and girls, are so deprived of the richness of loving that they are condemned to the poverty of the masturbation fantasy. Do we love our children in the right way? Are our schools kindly and human enough? Are our marriages real and satisfying?

Third, recognise quite simply and without breast-beating (we can't help it) the areas within us which are sick and have been so since babyhood. It is this recognition alone which gives us some control over the way we actually live — it is this, I often think, that is meant by free-will; and, in the degree to which we dare to face our own pathology, to that degree we can prevent it spilling over and making a mess of our own lives and of others. We are not angels, and there is no reason for us to pretend to be so; I have one sort of sickness, you have another.

In all of this pornography is in a sense neutral, meaningful to us or not, upsetting or not. It is a sad phenomenon, constantly reminding us, as individuals and as a society, that we have failed. If, however, we can use its existence as a departure-point for the understanding, and healing, of our society, then even pornography can be used for a positive purpose.

8: Ideals and Idols

IMAGINE A GROUP of people who had begun to worship an idol. They, of course, would not perceive that it was an idol — no one knowingly worships an idol — but would insist that this image represented the true God, and that the laws that came from him were the true laws. The Old Testament has terrifying examples of idols who ordered men to mutilate themselves or destroy themselves or their children.

But how, one might ask, could idols 'order' or 'make laws' at all, since they were made of wood and stone and could not speak nor move men's minds to creative impulses? What seems to happen is that man hears an inner voice and believes it comes from the idol. Unlike the creative voice *this* voice tells him that he must suffer to the point of self-destruction, or that he must insist upon courses of action that will destroy others. Relentlessly inflexible, the voice of the idol projects what is most harsh, ashamed and unforgiving in men, unforgiving of themselves and unforgiving of others.

Of course, not all idols are as bloodthirsty as the Baals and Molochs of the Old Testament. The Pharisees of Christ's time had constructed a different sort of idol for themselves. Working upon what we should call the 'obsessional' trait in the Jewish character, their idol made religion a matter of getting interminable details correct. There were so many tiny rituals to be remembered, such over-scrupulous decisions about the 'rightness' of the tiniest everyday actions, that no normal person with a living to earn could hope to be 'religious' at all.

It was a full-time occupation; and even then, however hard you tried, you probably didn't get it right. 'Ordinary' people, with their customary good sense, abandoned the struggle to lead devout lives for the very good reason that the Pharisees had, as Christ put it, laid a burden upon them too great to be borne. Once again the harshness and inflexibility of the idol shut out the vision of the true God.

Man, I suspect, is a compulsive maker of idols. Give us a bit of clay — the clay of our shame and our guilt and our fear of our darkest impulses — and in no time at all we will fashion a cruel face to warn us and rebuke us and punish us until we have reduced our inner world, and the world around us, to a desert. Our world abounds in racial and political idols who insist that men must be tortured, shot, blown up, maimed or killed to appease the inner Moloch.

It would be nice if we Christians were exempt from idol-making, but of course we are not; and, like all human groups, the place where we secrete our idol is at the very heart of all we hold most dear, in the midst of the beliefs of which we are most proud. I want to make the suggestion that our idol is what we usually dub our 'Christian ideals', and that it has the most power in the area of our sexual ideals.

Ideals are a sort of vision of how things might be in a perfect world, and they are so beautiful and so seductive that we forget it never has been like that, and never will be. Ideals are, so we think, how things *ought* to be; and, because this gives us a warm glow inside, we try very hard to make ourselves and others fit the formula — the way old Procrustes tried to make his visitors fit his bed.

Annoyingly, we don't fit at all well. In some cases there is too much of us and we hang over the ends of the bed; Procrustes's solution was to chop off recalcitrant members. Others are too short and have to be stretched on the rack. If you don't fit the Christian sexual ideal, try as you will, the choice seems to be between being mutilated or tortured.

You will now be muttering (I hope), 'Unfair, unfair!' for, whereas the laws of Moloch or even the fal-de-lals of the Pharisees were man's self-destructive voice talking, our 'Christian ideals' are the very voice of love itself. Abstinence from sex before marriage (and no masturbation either), total fidelity within marriage whatever the relationship may turn out to be like, heterosex not homosex, renunciation of all unloving fantasies, *are* the best way of living with our rather stormy sexual natures.

To which I would want to reply, 'Yes and no.' Yes, because I think it may be that, when a man or woman reaches emotional maturity, absolute fidelity to a person of the opposite sex may represent for them the ultimate satisfaction and fulfilment. No, because it takes some of us many years to achieve emotional maturity, and many of us never make it, and in the meantime it is not always the best or the honest or even the possible course to pant after an ideal that is beyond us and spurn the more mundane ways of love and growth that are within our power.

If, in fact, the Christians are insisting upon an ideal that is beyond most people, then they are doing what the Pharisees did, and binding upon men burdens too great to be borne. And this has the same tragic effect that 'ordinary' people cease to take seriously the religious insights that do come their way.

For example, if a man or a woman discovers that his experience of God comes to him or her through an affair, either heterosexual or homosexual, or even through his marriage to a divorced person, what sense can he make of a Church which teaches that this cannot be so? And what hope has the Church of making anything of him?

My own belief is that the way forward is for a new courage and flexibility and generosity among Christians, more particularly towards the forms of sexuality that have frightened them most in the past, and more particularly still towards the echoes of the same sexuality in themselves. The alternative, I have come to believe, is a mutilating and destroying of the human personality less dramatic but no less terrible than the 'commands' of Moloch.